CHILDREN'S ATLAS

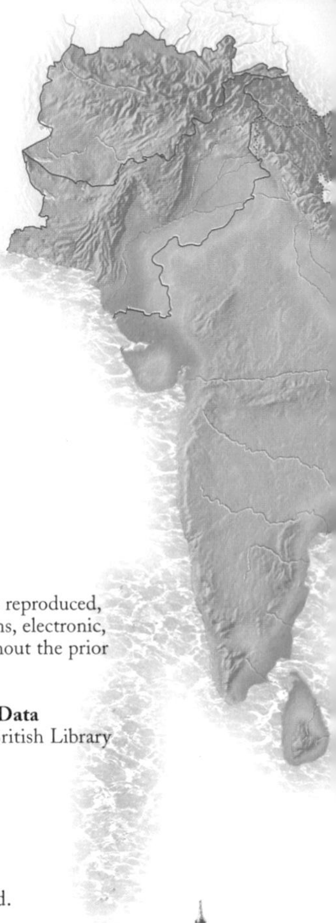

This is a Parragon Book
This edition published in 2001

Parragon
Queen Street House
4 Queen Street
Bath BA1 1HE, UK

2 4 6 8 10 9 7 5 3 1

Produced by
Miles Kelly Publishing Ltd.

British Library Cataloguing-in-Publication Data
A catalogue record for this book is available from the British Library

Printed in Italy

ISBN 0-75256-360-2

Cover Design: Miles Kelly Publishing Ltd.

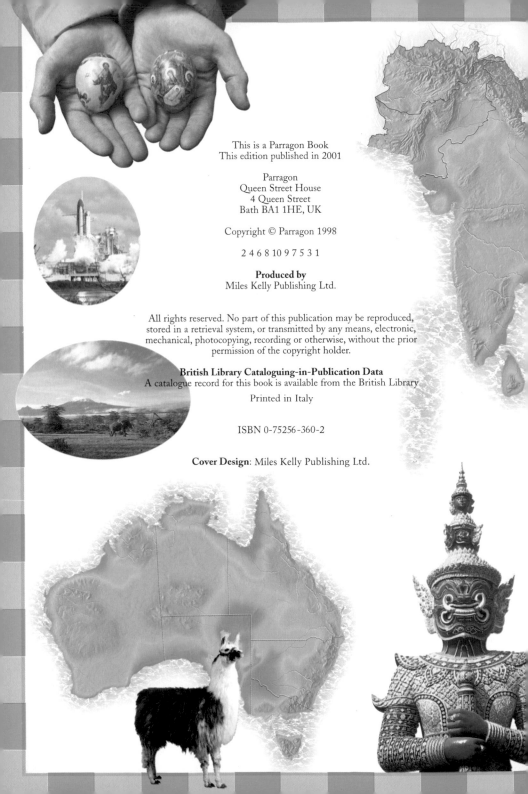

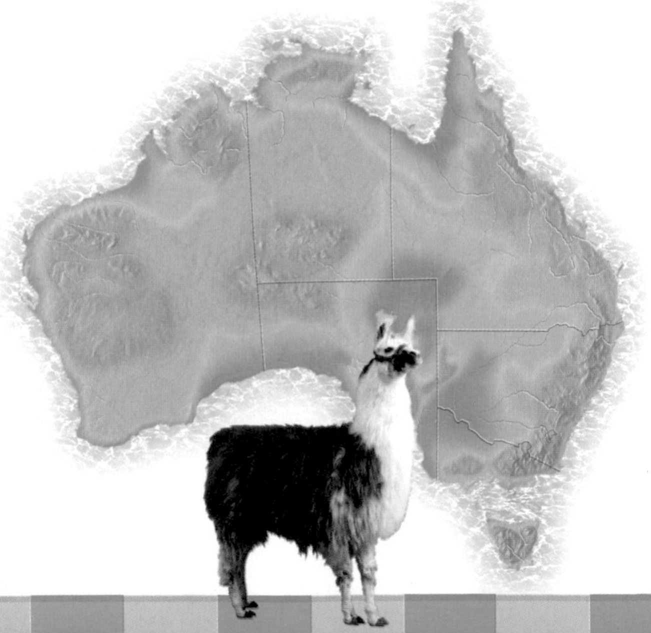

CONTENTS

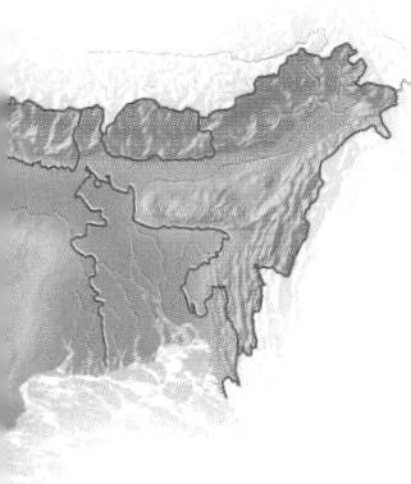

HOW TO USE THIS ATLAS

WELCOME TO THE PLANET EARTH! This atlas shows you the world we live in. An atlas is any large book of maps. Maps are plans which show the surface of a planet as if it was flat, instead of round. They show the lie of the land, the rivers and coastlines, mountains and seas.

Maps which just show the details of the landscape are called 'physical'. Maps which just show the borders of countries, states, counties or provinces are called 'political'. The maps in this book show the physical details of the land, but they show national borders and major cities as well. Maps use signs and symbols to give you more information. Look at the key to find out what they mean.

So how do you find the city or country you are looking for? First of all look up the name you want in the index on p.61. When you have found the right page, look for the name on the big map of the region. Next to each regional map, look for the little map which helps you to see at a glance which part of the world is being shown.

Next, read the words to find out more about the countries, the climate of the region, the peoples and how they live. Small boxes also give you key facts and figures about each of the countries. They tell you the area, the population size, the name of the capital city, the country's official language or languages and the currency, or type of money, used by the people there.

When you read about distant lands, it may help to compare them with where you live. Are they bigger or smaller, hotter or wetter, more crowded? You might use the maps to do a bit of detective work. Can you work out why most Australian cities are near the coast, or why most Canadian cities are in the south of the country?

Colours
On this map the different colours show you at a glance the physical features of the landscape. Each colour represents a type of geographic feature.

Spot the mountain
This symbol means 'mountain'. The mountain's name is printed next to it, along with the height of the summit above sea level. The height is given in metres.

N for north
This symbol represents a compass, with its magnetic needle pointing due north.

Coastlines and borders
The borders of Japan are natural, because the country is made up of islands. Other countries may have land borders, marked by a line on the map.

Capital cities
The most important town in any country is called the capital city. This is very often the biggest town and is normally where the government makes the laws. Some capitals, however, are quite small.

Where in the world
If you want to find out where the regional map fits into a map of the whole world, check these small circular maps. The areas coloured in red show the location.

Key to symbols

■	Capitals
●	Towns
—	Rivers
—	Borders
	Lakes
	Mountains

INTRODUCTION

EARTH FACTS

The world we live in is a huge ball of rock and metal spinning around, or rotating, in space. As the planet Earth rotates, it travels around the Sun, held on its path by a pulling force called gravity. The Earth is one of nine planets circling the Sun, and together they make up the Solar System.

When we see pictures of Earth taken from space, our planet appears blue, white and brown. The blue is the colour of the seas and oceans which cover over two-thirds of the Earth's surface. The swirling white patterns are the clouds – water vapour which hangs in the air, or atmosphere, surrounding the Earth's surface. The brown is the colour of the ground, which is divided into the Earth's landmasses or continents.

Photographs of the Earth's surface taken from space zoom in to show even more details – the world's great river systems, the high mountain ranges, the sprawling cities and the patchwork of crops that feed the hungry mouths of the world's population, which is expected to reach over 6,100 million by the year 2000.

PLANET EARTH

Circumference around the Equator: 40,075 kilometres
Circumference around the Poles: 40,008 kilometres
Diameter at the Equator: 12,756 kilometres
Surface area: About 510,000,000 square kilometres
Area covered by sea: 71 percent
Average distance from the Sun: 149,600,000 kilometres
Average distance from the Moon: 385,000 kilometres
Period of rotation: 23 hours 56 minutes
Speed of rotation: 1,660 kilometres per hour at the Equator
Period of revolution: 365 days 6 hours
Speed of revolution: 29.8 kilometres per second

FACT BOX

The world's highest peak
Mount Everest or Qomolangma, between Nepal and China, is the highest point on the Earth's surface.

HIGHEST PEAKS

Mountain	Height	Location
Everest (Qomolangma)	8,848 m	China-Nepal
K2 (Qogir Feng)	8,611 m	India-Pakistan
Kanchenjunga	8,586 m	India-Nepal
Makalu 1	8,463 m	China-Nepal
Dhaulagiri 1	8,167 m	Nepal
Nanga Parbat	8,125 m	India
Annapurna 1	8,091 m	Nepal
Gosainthan (Xixabangma Feng)	8,012 m	China
Distaghil Sar	7,885 m	India
Nanda Devi	7,816 m	India

LONGEST RIVERS

River	Length	Location
Nile	6,670 km	North Africa
Amazon	6,448 km	South America
Chang Jiang (Yangtze)	6,300 km	Central China
Mississippi-Missouri-Red	6,020 km	North America
Yenisey-Angara-Selenga	5,540 km	Mongolia-Russia
Huang He	5,464 km	Northern China
Ob-Irtysh	5,409 km	Russia-Kazakhstan
Zaïre (Congo)	4,700 km	Central Africa
Lena-Kirenga	4,400 km	Russia
Mekong	4,350 km	Southeast Asia

LARGEST LAKES

Lake	Area	Location
Caspian Sea	371,800 sq km	Central Asia
Superior	82,103 sq km	USA-Canada
Victoria	69,484 sq km	East Africa
Aral Sea	65,500 sq km	Central Asia
Huron	59,569 sq km	USA-Canada
Michigan	57,757 sq km	USA-Canada
Tanganyika	32,893 sq km	East Africa
Baikal	31,449 sq km	Russia
Great Bear	31,328 sq km	Canada
Malawi	28,878 sq km	Southern Africa

LARGEST ISLANDS

Island	Area
Greenland	2,1830 sq km
New Guinea	821,000 sq km
Borneo	727,900 sq km
Madagascar	589,081 sq km
Baffin	509,214 sq km
Sumatra	431,982 sq km
Honshu	228,204 sq km
Great Britain	218,800 sq km
Victoria	212,200 sq km
Ellesmere	196,917 sq km

MAJOR WATERFALLS

Highest Waterfalls	Height	Location
Angel Falls	979 m	Venezuela
Mardsalsfossen	774 m	Norway
Yosemite	739 m	United States

Greatest volume

Waterfall	Volume	Location
Boyoma	17,000 cu m per sec	Dem. Rep. Congo (Zaïre)

OCEANS

Name	Area
Pacific	166,242,000 sq km
Atlantic	106,000,000 sq km
Indian	73,500,000 sq km
Arctic	14,350,000 sq km

COUNTRIES OF THE WORLD

To the glory of God
Places of worship vary greatly around the world. This Christian cathedral, St Basil's, was built in the 1500s in Moscow, capital of today's Russian Federation.

There are 192 countries in the world that are recognized as 'independent' nations, which means that they govern themselves. Many other lands are colonies or 'dependencies', which means that they are governed by other nations. The numbers change very often, as one country joins up with another one, or another splits up into separate nations. For example Eritrea was part of Ethiopia until 1991, when it broke away to become an independent nation.

Some countries are huge, some are tiny. The Russian Federation is the largest, with an area of 17,078,005 square kilometres. The smallest is Vatican City, at just 0.4 square kilometres. Some countries are home to just one people, while others are made up of many different peoples or ethnic groups, each with their own way of life and customs. Some people have no national borders of their own. For example the traditional homeland of the Kurdish people is divided between Turkey, Iraq and Iran.

The peoples of the world live very different lives. They have different faiths and beliefs, eat different foods and speak over 5000 different languages. Some people are very poor while others are very rich. However, the people on our planet also have many things in common. The spread of radio, television and other communications links in recent years has made the world a smaller place. Once it took years to travel around the world, but today we can get on a plane or keep in touch with each other at the push of a button.

Most of the world's countries are linked by agreements or treaties. Many European countries belong to the European Union, while African nations belong to the Organization of African Unity. Nearly all countries belong to the United Nations, which tries to prevent conflict and to build links between the world's nations.

Political power
These heads, cut from the rock at Mount Rushmore, USA, honour US presidents - George Washington, Thomas Jefferson, Theodore Roosevelt and Abraham Lincoln.

Trade and commerce
It is said that 'money makes the world go round'. These bright lights are in the Kowloon district of Hong Kong, a former British colony that returned to Chinese rule in 1997.

Cooking around the world
Pizza is made of a doughy pastry topped by cheese, tomato, vegetables, herbs and sausage. This Italian dish is now very popular in many parts of the world.

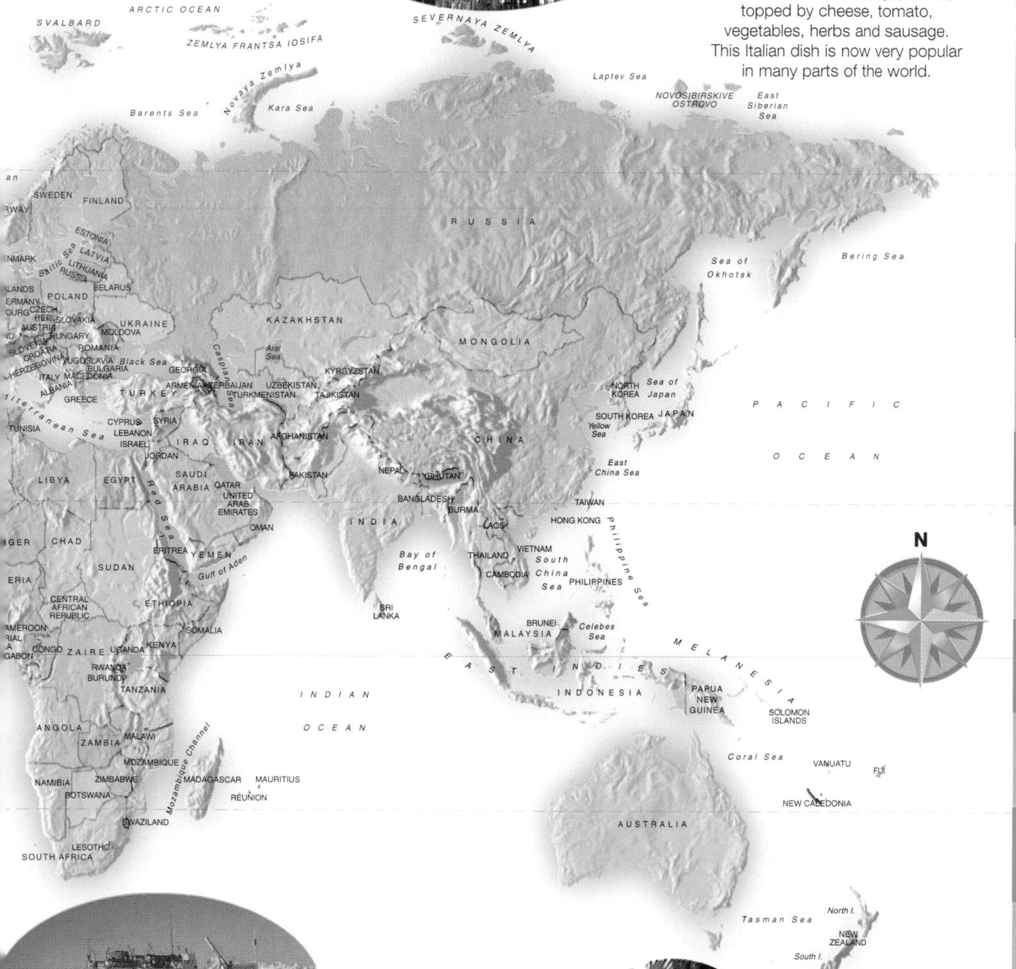

Save the wilderness
This ship is entering pack ice off the coast of Antarctica. Nobody lives in this freezing continent at the bottom of the world. It is one of the last few wild places on Earth.

Peoples and customs
Traditional body paint and costume are worn for this dance in Papua New Guinea. Regional dress has become less common around the world in recent years, but is still worn with pride for special ceremonies.

EUROPE

SCANDINAVIA AND FINLAND

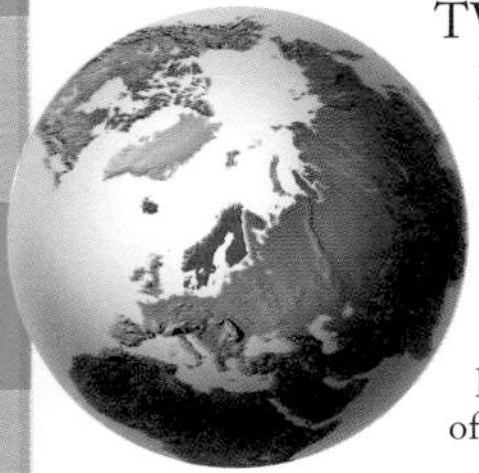

TWO PENINSULAS extend from northwestern Europe, shaped rather like the claws of a crab. The southern peninsula, extending from Germany, is called Jutland.

Together with a chain of islands which includes Fyn, Sjælland, and Lolland, Jutland makes up the nation of **Denmark**. Most of Denmark is flat and low-lying, a country of green farmland. It exports bacon and dairy products.

Across the windy channels of Sgagerrak and Kattegat, between the North and Baltic Seas, lies the long northern peninsula occupied by **Sweden** and **Norway**. This is a land shaped by movements of ice in prehistoric times. Glaciers carved out the deep sea inlets called fjords along its ragged western coast. Ranges of mountains run down the peninsula like a backbone. They descend to a land of forests, bogs and thousands of lakes.

Summers can be warm, but winters are bitterly cold, with heavy snow. Norway lives by fishing and its North Sea rigs make it Western Europe's largest producer of oil and natural gas. Sweden is a major exporter of timber, paper, wooden furniture and motor vehicles.

The three nations of Denmark, Sweden and Norway form the region of Scandinavia. It was from here that the seafarers known as Vikings set out about 1,200 years ago. The Vikings raided and settled the coasts of Western Europe, traded in Russia and the Middle East, settled Iceland and Greenland and even reached North America. Today's Danes, Swedes and Norwegians are all closely related, as are the Germanic languages that they speak.

The Arctic lands of northern Scandinavia are home to the Saami (or Lapps), a people who traditionally lived by herding reindeer. Their neighbours are the Finns and the Russians.

Finland is a land of lakes, with coasts on the Gulfs of Bothnia and Finland. Its forests make it a leading producer

FACT BOX

◆ **Denmark**
Area: 43,075 sq km
Population: 5,300,000
Capital: Copenhagen
Official language: Danish
Currency: Danish krone

◆ **Sweden**
Area: 449,790 sq km
Population: 8,000,000
Capital: Stockholm
Official language: Swedish
Currency: Krona

◆ **Norway**
Area: 323,895 sq km
Population: 4,400,000
Capital: Oslo
Official language: Norwegian
Currency: Norwegian krone

◆ **Finland**
Area: 337,030 sq km
Population: 5,100,000
Capital: Helsinki
Official language: Finnish
Currency: Markka

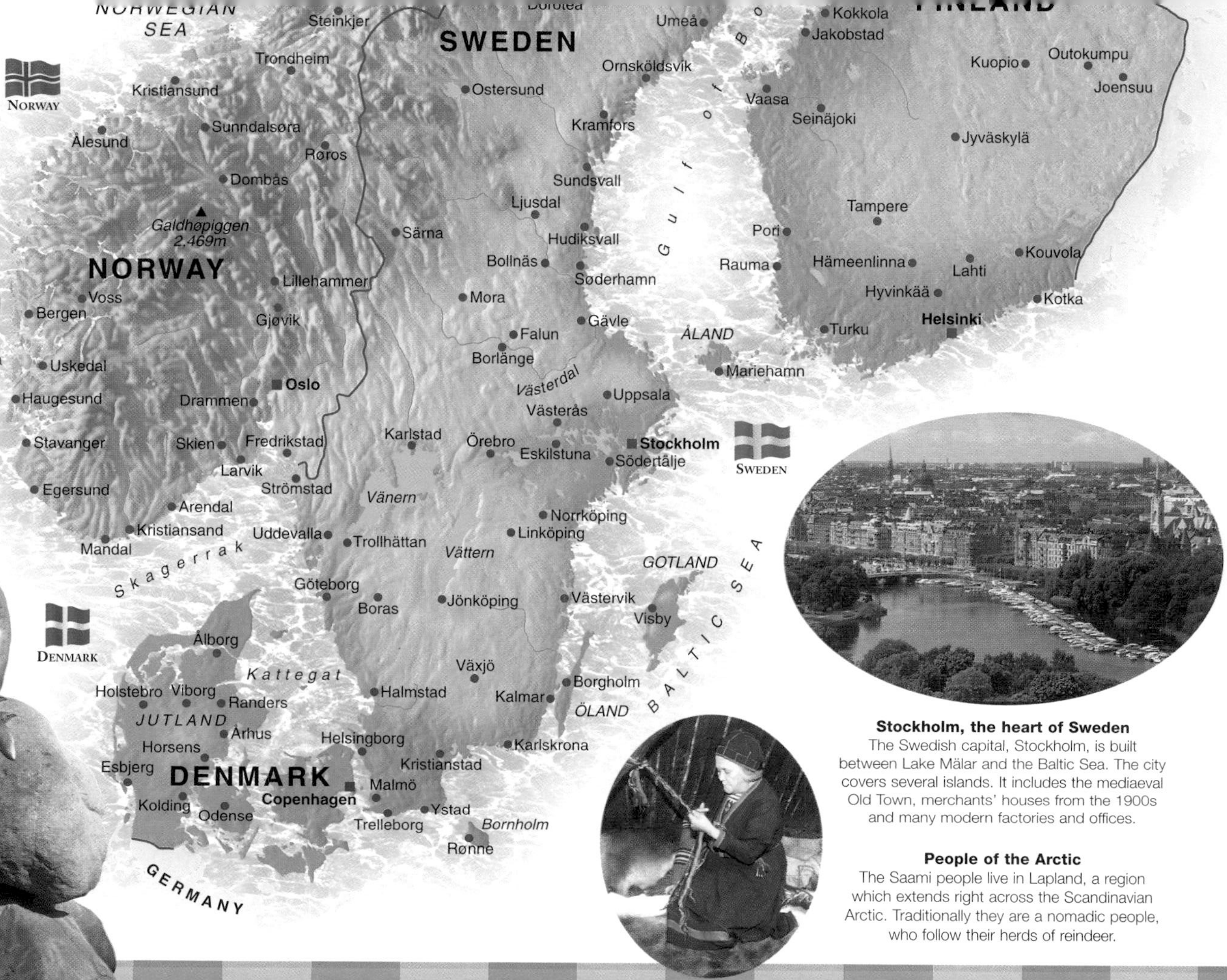

The Little Mermaid
This bronze statue in the Danish capital, Copenhagen, shows a character from one of the children's stories by Hans Christian Andersen (1805-75). Andersen created some of the world's best loved fairy tales.

Stockholm, the heart of Sweden
The Swedish capital, Stockholm, is built between Lake Mälar and the Baltic Sea. The city covers several islands. It includes the mediaeval Old Town, merchants' houses from the 1900s and many modern factories and offices.

People of the Arctic
The Saami people live in Lapland, a region which extends right across the Scandinavian Arctic. Traditionally they are a nomadic people, who follow their herds of reindeer.

EUROPE

LOW COUNTRIES

THE COUNTRY OF THE NETHERLANDS is sometimes called Holland, but that is really the name of just two of its provinces, North and South Holland. This is a very flat, low-lying part of northern Europe. Long barriers and sea walls have been built to protect the countryside from North Sea floods. Large areas of land called polders have been reclaimed from the sea over the ages.

After a period under Spanish rule, the **Netherlands** became wealthy in the 1600s by trading with Southeast Asia. Its capital city, Amsterdam, still has many beautiful old houses and canals dating back to this golden age. The Netherlands today remain a centre of commerce, exporting bulbs and cut flowers, vegetables and dairy products, especially cheese, and also electrical goods. Rotterdam is the world's busiest seaport. Peoples of the Netherlands include the Dutch and the Frisians, as well as people whose families came from former Dutch colonies in Indonesia and Surinam.

The Flemish people of **Belgium** are closely related to the Dutch and their two languages are very similar. Belgium is also home to a French-speaking people, the Walloons, who mostly live in the south of the country. Much of the countryside in Belgium is also low and flat, but the land rises to the wooded hills of the Ardennes in the south. The country is heavily industrialized. and is also known for its fine foods – chocolates, pâtés, hams and traditional beers.

Luxembourg is a tiny country, a survivor of the age when most of Europe was divided into little states, principalities and duchies. However, modern industry and banking have made Luxembourg wealthy and successful. The people of Luxembourg speak French, German and a local language called Letzebuergesch.

The three countries have close ties. In 1948, after the terrible years of World War II (1939-45), Belgium, the Netherlands and Luxembourg set up an economic union called 'Benelux'. In 1957 they went on to what is now the European Union (EU).

Bruges skyline

The brick gables of old merchants' houses make a pleasing skyline in many historical towns of the Lowlands. Bruges has been famous through the ages for its lacemaking. The city is linked by canal to the seaport of Zeebrugge.

FACT BOX

◆ **Netherlands**
Area: 41,160 sq km
Population: 15,600,000
Capital: Amsterdam
Official language: Dutch
Currency: Guilder

◆ **Belgium**
Area: 30,520 sq km
Population: 10,200,000
Capital: Brussels
Official languages: Flemish, French
Currency: Belgian franc

◆ **Luxembourg**
Area: 2,585 sq km
Population: 400,000
Capital: Luxembourg
Official language: French, German, Letzebuergesch
Currency: Luxembourg franc

Wetlands butterfly

The Large Copper butterfly is on the endangered species list in both Belgium and the Netherlands. The butterfly thrives in flooded fields. Its caterpillar can survive underwater for many weeks. However draining of wetlands by farmers and roadbuilders threatens its survival.

'When it's spring again...'
The classic Dutch landscape includes fields of brilliantly coloured tulips and old-fashioned windmills. Both attract the tourists and are seen here near the town of Haarlem.

Dutch cheese
Another popular attraction in the Netherlands is the cheese market at Alkmaar. The Netherlands exports mild cheeses such as Edam and Gouda around the world.

The future – 1958 style
This strange looking landmark is the Atomium. It was built for the World Fair held in Brussels in 1958 and was meant to be a symbol of a new age of atomic science and technology.

EUROPE

BRITISH ISLES

THE BRITISH ISLES lie off the northwestern coast of Europe, between the shallow waters of the North Sea and the stormy Atlantic Ocean. Their western shores are warmed by an ocean current called the North Atlantic Drift. The climate is mild, with a high rainfall in the west.

The largest island is called **Great Britain**, and its three countries (**England, Scotland** and **Wales**) are joined together within a United Kingdom. The second largest of the British Isles is called **Ireland**. Most of Ireland is an independent republic, but part of the north is governed as a province of the United Kingdom.

Great Britain has a landscape of rolling farmland. There are rugged highlands in Wales and Scotland, while England has rich farmland in the southeast, bleak moors in the north, flat fields in East Anglia and wild coasts in Cornwall. There are many beautiful old villages and towns, but also large cities and ports.

The Irish landscape is less crowded. It has green fields, misty hills and, in the west, steep cliffs pounded by Atlantic breakers. Its capital, Dublin, lies on the River Liffey.

English is spoken throughout the British Isles, but other languages may be heard too – Welsh, Irish and Scots Gaelic, and the various languages spoken by British people of Asian and African descent.

Both the UK and the **Republic of Ireland** are members of the

Wren
One of the most widespread birds of Britain, this short drab coloured bird with a cocked tail, has a loud warbling song. Wrens feed on caterpillars, beetles and bugs.

FACT BOX

◆ **United Kingdom: England, Scotland, Wales, N. Ireland**
Area: 242,480 sq km
Population: 58,000,000
Capital: London
Official language: English
Currency: Sterling pound

◆ **England**
Area: 130,420 sq km
Population: 48,675,119
Capital: London
Official language: English
Currency: Sterling pound

◆ **Scotland**
Area: 77,170 sq km
Population: 5,111,000
Capital: Edinburgh
Official language: English
Currency: Sterling pound

◆ **Wales**
Area: 20,770 sq km
Population: 2,899,000
Capital: Cardiff
Official language: Welsh, English
Currency: Sterling pound

◆ **Northern Ireland**
Area: 14,150 sq km
Population: 1,610,000
Capital: Belfast
Official language: English
Currency: Sterling pound

◆ **Republic of Ireland**
Area: 70,283 sq km
Population: 3,552,000
Capital: Dublin
Official language: English, Irish
Currency: Irish pound (punt)

Highland games
Scottish pipers parade in the Highland Games. This competition has been taking place since the early nineteenth century, but has its roots

Ladies' View, Killarney, Eire

This famous beauty spot in southern Ireland enjoys wonderful views of Macgillycuddyís Reeks (a mountain range) and the lakes of Killarney. Of these lakes Lough Learne, or lower lake, is the largest with over 30 islands.

Tower of London

Built in the eleventh century by William the Conqueror, this ancient fortress on the river Thames was once a royal home. It is now a museum and houses the crown jewels. It was here that Anne Boleyn, wife of Henry VIII, was beheaded. Yeomen of the Guard, or Beefeaters, still guard the Tower.

FRANCE AND MONACO

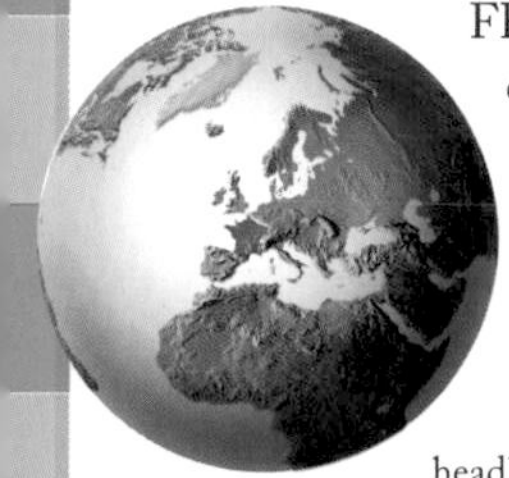

FRANCE IS A LARGE, beautiful country which lies at the heart of Western Europe. Its western regions include the massive peaks of the Pyrenees, vineyards and pine forests, peaceful rivers and Atlantic shores.

The north includes the stormy headlands of Brittany, the cliffs of Normandy and the Channel ports. Rolling fertile plains are drained by the winding river Seine, over whose banks and islands sprawls the French capital. Paris is one of the world's great cities, with broad avenues, historic palaces and churches.

The west of **France** is bordered by wooded hills which rise to the high forested slopes of the Jura mountains and finally the spectacular glaciers and ridges of the Alps. The rocks of the Massif Central, shaped by ancient volcanoes, rise in central southern France, to the west of the Rhône valley. The sun-baked hills of southern France border the warm seas of the Mediterranean Sea. This coast includes the wetlands of the Camargue, the great seaport of Marseilles and the fashionable yachting marinas of Cannes.

France has played a major part in history, and the French language is now spoken in many parts of the world. The French people are mostly descended from a Celtic people called the Gauls and Germanic peoples, such as the Franks and Vikings. Within France are several other peoples with their own languages and distinct cultures, such as Bretons, Basques, Catalans, Alsatians, Corsicans and Algerians.

France is a republic belonging to the European Union (EU) and is an important industrial power, producing cars, aerospace equipment, chemicals and textiles. The country is renowned for its wines, its cheeses, and its fine cooking.

Part of the Mediterranean coast is occupied by a very small principality called **Monaco**. It has close links with its large neighbour and shares the same currency. The state is famous for its casino.

Château de Charumont
France has many historical castles, palaces and stately homes, or châteaux. Some of the finest are in the Loire valley.

Sacré-Coeur
The gleaming domes of this church soar above the Parisian district of Montmartre, once famed as the haunt of artists and writers.

Shape of the future
The Futuroscope theme park and study centre, near Poitiers, is one example of France's many experimental modern buildings. This theatre looks like a huge crystal.

Vineyard harvest
Grapes are gathered at a vineyard in Alsace, on the slopes of the Vosges. Grapes, grown in many regions of France, are made into some of the world's finest wines.

Fact Box

◆ **France**
Area: 543,965 sq km
Population: 58,600,000
Capital: Paris
Official language: French
Currency: French franc

◆ **Monaco**
Area: 1.9 sq km
Population: 28,000
Capital: Monaco
Official language: French
Currency: French franc

Quiche Lorraine
A speciality of north-eastern France, this is a baked pastry tart filled with eggs, cream, cheese and bacon.

Fact Box

◆ **Germany**
Area: 356,840sq km
Population: 82,000,000
Capital: Berlin
Official language: German
Currency: Deutsche mark

◆ **Switzerland**
Area: 41,285 sq km
Population: 7,100,000
Capital: Bern
Official languages: German, French, Italian, Romansh
Currency: Swiss franc

◆ **Liechtenstein**
Area: 160 sq km
Population: 30,000
Capital: Vaduz
Official language: German
Currency: Swiss franc

◆ **Austria**
Area: 83,855 sq km
Population: 8,100,000
Capital: Vienna
Official language: German
Currency: Schilling

GERMANY & THE ALPS

GERMANY LIES BETWEEN Western and Central Europe. In the south the high peaks of the Alps are flanked by belts of forest.

The rolling hills and heathland of the centre stretch to the North Sea, while in the west the rivers Rhine and Moselle wind through steep valleys planted with vines. In the northeast a vast plain is bordered by the Baltic Sea and by the rivers Oder and Neisse.

For most of its history Germany has been divided into different states. Today's united Germany dates from 1990. Germany is a federal republic, which means that its regions or Länder have considerable powers. The country is a leading member of the European Union and is a major world producer of cars, electrical and household goods, medicines, chemicals, wines and beers.

Switzerland is a small country set amongst the lakes and snowy peaks of the Alps and the Jura ranges. Its beautiful landscape and historical towns attract many tourists. Industries include dairy produce, precision instruments and finance. Zurich is a world centre of banking, while Geneva is the headquarters of many international agencies, such as the Red Cross and the World Health Organization.

To the east, the tiny country of **Liechtenstein** is closely linked with Switzerland and uses the same currency. The land of **Austria** descends from the soaring peaks of the Alps to the flat lands of the Danube river valley. Austria once ruled a large empire which stretched eastwards into Hungary and southwards into Italy. Today Austria still plays an important part in Europe, making its living from tourism, farming, forestry and manufacture.

German is spoken through most of the region, with a great variety of dialects. In parts of Switzerland there are people who speak French, Italian and Romansh.

Edelweiss
This small herb, with its pretty white flower, grows in the European Alps. High mountain meadows are filled with wildflowers in spring and summer.

Brimming with beer
Munich, capital of Bavaria in southern Germany, hosts a famous beer festival every October. Regional dress is still common in the region.

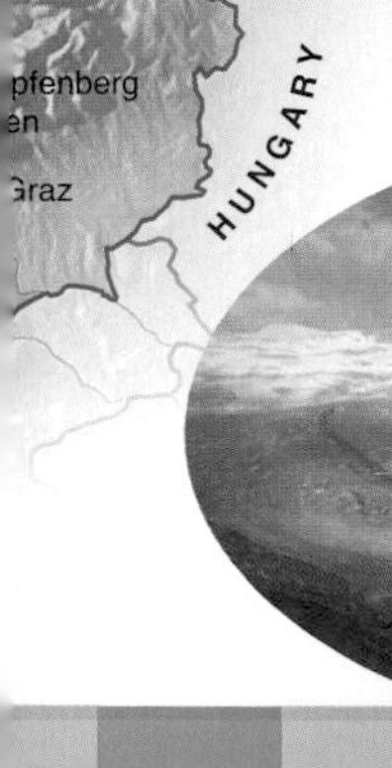

River of ice
This impressive glacier grinds its way down the Alps near Zermatt. Many tourists and climbers visit Switzerland to enjoy the spectacular views.

Medieval revelry
Festival costumes recall the Middle Ages in Baden Württemberg. During that period Germany was made up of many small states.

IBERIAN PENINSULA

THE IBERIAN PENINSULA is in southwestern Europe, and juts out into the Atlantic Ocean. It is bordered to the north by the stormy Bay of Biscay and to the south by the Mediterranean Sea and the Balearic Islands. Across the Strait of Gibraltar, just 13 kilometres away, lies the continent of Africa.

The north coast, green from high rainfall, rises to the Cantabrian mountains, while the snowy Pyrenees form a high barrier along the Spanish-French frontier. Another range, the Sierra Nevada, runs parallel with the south coast. Inland, much of the Iberian peninsula is taken up by an extremely dry, rocky plateau, which swelters in the heat of summer. To the west are forested highlands and the fertile plains of Portugal, crossed by great rivers such as the Douro, Tagus and Guadiana.

The Iberian peninsula is occupied by four countries or territories. There is **Gibraltar**, a British colony since 1713, and the tiny independent state of **Andorra**, high in the Pyrenees. The two main countries of the region are **Spain** and **Portugal**. Both have a history of overseas settlement, and both Spanish and Portuguese have become the chief languages of Latin America. Many people speak other languages, including Basque and Catalan, and have their own traditions and history.

Both Spain and Portugal were ruled by dictators for much of the 20th century, but today both are democracies and members of the European Union. Spain produces olives, citrus fruits, wines and sherries, and has a large fishing fleet. Portugal also produces wine and port takes its name from the city of Oporto. Fishing villages line the coasts and cork, used for bottle stoppers and tiling, is cut from the thick bark of the cork oak tree.

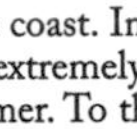

PORTUGAL

Feria in Seville

At the Feria, held in the Spanish city of Seville every April, people ride into town dressed in traditional finery. The river is lined with tents and pavilions. The festival is celebrated with bullfights, flamenco music and dancing.

Fishing boats, Nazaré
Fishing boats line the beach at Nazaré, on the Portuguese coast. The fishermen brave the Atlantic waves daily in their search for the sardines and tuna that make up their catch.

FACT BOX

◆ **Spain**
Area: 504,880 sq km
Population: 39,300,000
Capital: Madrid
Official language: Spanish
Currency: Peseta

◆ **Portugal**
Area: 91,630 sq km
Population: 9,900,000
Capital: Lisbon
Official language: Portuguese
Currency: Escudo

◆ **Andorra**
Area: 465 sq km
Population: 62,000
Capital: Andorra la Vella
Official language: Catalan
Currency: French franc, Spanish peseta

Portuguese explorers
This monument is in Lisbon, the Portuguese capital. It honours the Portuguese seafarers who were among the first Europeans to explore the coasts of Africa, Asia and the Americas. Prince Henry (1394–1460) founded the first school of navigation.

Spanish paella
Paella takes its name from the large pan in which it is cooked. It is made of rice with saffron and garlic, mixed with prawns and other seafoods, vegetables, chicken or ham.

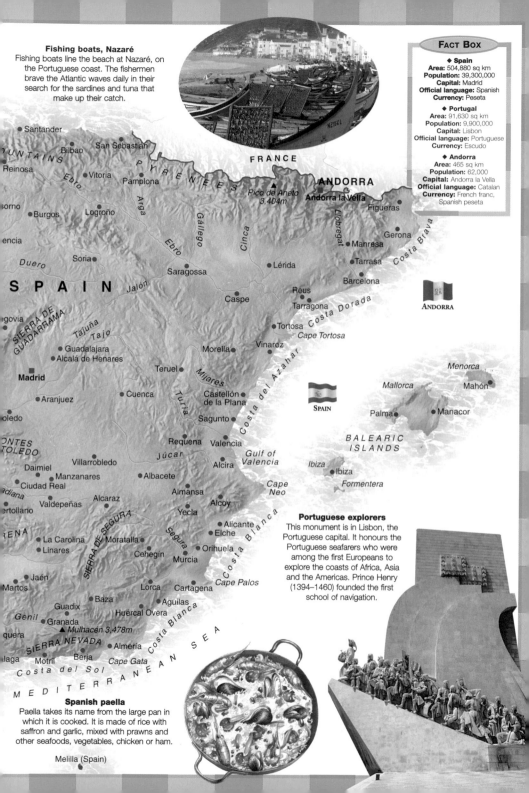

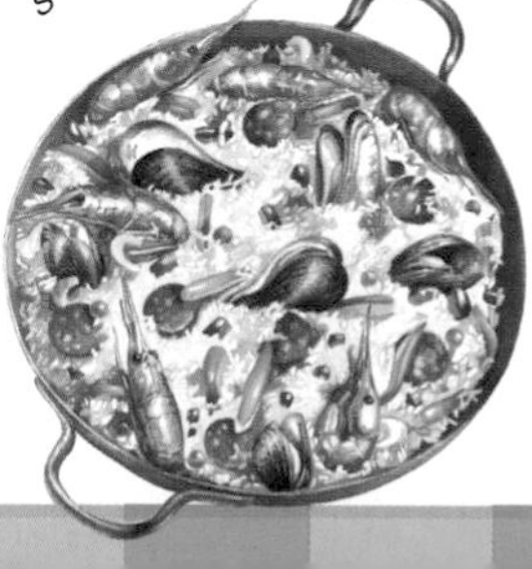

ITALY AND ITS NEIGHBOURS

Spaghetti Bolognese
Spaghetti is a kind of pasta. Made from wheat and eggs, pasta is eaten in all kinds of shapes and sizes, each with its own name. Here it is served with a meat and tomato sauce, invented in the city of Bologna. Italians who have left their homeland have made their cooking popular around the world.

Sun and sea
Portofino is a small town on the Gulf of Genoa, in Italy's Liguria region. Its pretty waterfront and fishing boats attract many tourists in the hot Mediterranean summer.

ITALY OCCUPIES a long, boot-shaped peninsula which stretches south from the snowy peaks and blue lakes of the Alps into the Mediterranean Sea. The country also takes in the large islands of Sardinia and Sicily. The northern regions of the mainland include the wide, fertile plains around the river Po and wealthy industrial cities.

A long chain of mountains, the Appenines, run down the spine of **Italy**. They descend to coastal farmland and the hot, dry plains of the south. Southern Italy and its islands are one of the world's volcanic danger zones.

Olives and grapes grow well in its sunny climate and Italy is the largest wine producer in the world. Factories produce cars, textiles and leather goods.

Modern Italy has only been united since 1861, but in ancient times Rome was the capital of a vast empire which stretched across western Europe, southwest Asia and North Africa. Rome later became the centre of the Catholic Church and during the 1400s and 1500s cities such as Florence saw a great flowering of scholarship and the arts, known as the Renaissance. Many tourists visit Italy to see its ancient sites.

Italian, based on the ancient Latin language, is spoken throughout Italy, but in border regions you may hear other languages – French, German or Slovenian. The Ladin language is spoken in the Dolomite mountains and the people of Sardinia speak their own ancient dialect of Italian.

Two small independent states lie entirely surrounded by Italian territory. One is the world's smallest country, known as **Vatican City**. It is a district of Rome which serves as headquarters for the Pope and the Roman Catholic Church. The other is tiny **San Marino.**

South of Italy, towards the coast of North Africa is the chain of islands which make up **Malta**. The Maltese have their own language and live from building and repairing ships and from tourism.

ITALY

VATICAN CITY

The Leaning Tower
This famous marble bell tower was built in the Italian city of Pisa during the Middle Ages. Unfortunately, it was raised on unstable ground and soon began to sink. Today it leans over from the vertical by about 5 metres.

On the Gulf of Salerno
The seaport of Amalfi lies at the foot of Monte Cerreto, to the south-east of the city of Naples. The scenery here is spectacular.

Venice carnival
Elegant masks, cloaks and costumes in the style of the 1700s disguise revellers at Venice's famous carnival. Venice is one of the most beautiful cities in Europe.

FACT BOX

◆ **Italy**
Area: 301,245 sq km
Population: 57,100,000
Capital: Rome
Official language: Italian
Currency: Italian lira

◆ **Vatican City**
Area: 0.44 sq km
Population: 1,000
Official language: Latin
Currency: Italian lira

◆ **San Marino**
Area: 61 sq km
Population: 23,000
Capital: San Marino
Official language: Italian
Currency: Italian lira

◆ **Malta**
Area: 316 sq km
Population: 359,000
Capital: Valletta
Official languages: Maltese, English
Currency: Maltese lira

CENTRAL EUROPE

THREE SMALL COUNTRIES cluster around the eastern shores of the Baltic Sea. **Estonia**, **Latvia** and **Lithuania** were part of the Soviet Union (today's Russian Federation) from 1940 until 1991, when they became independent. Their lands include forests and lakes, farmland and industrial cities.

Poland, which has historic links with Lithuania, is a large country which has also known invasions and foreign rule through much of its history. Despite this, the Poles, a Slavic people, have kept a sense of independence and a pride in their traditions. The lands near Poland's Baltic coast are dotted with lakes. The north is a flat land of pine forests, part of the great plain which stretches from eastern Germany into Russia. It is cold and snowy in winter, but warm in summer. In southern Poland the land rises to highlands and the jagged peaks of the Tatra mountains, along the Slovakian border.

Slovakia and the **Czech Republic** were a single country until 1993. Slovakia is a land of high mountains dropping to fertile farmland around the River Danube, which forms its southeastern border. When the two countries divided, most industry lay on the Czech side of the border. The Czech Republic produces beer, glass, ceramics, steel and machinery. The country is bordered by mountains and, in the east, by the Bohemian centre of learning and the arts.

The Czechs and Slovaks are both Slavic peoples, but the Hungarians are Magyars, a people who invaded and settled in the region about 1200 years ago. **Hungary** is a country of wide open plains and low mountains. Its fertile farmland produces fruits, grains and grapes for making strong red wine. Its beautiful capital, Budapest, is on the River Danube.

FACT BOX

◆ **Poland**
Area: 312,685 sq km
Population: 38,600,000
Capital: Warsaw
Official language: Polish
Currency: Zloty

◆ **Czech Republic**
Area: 78,864 sq km
Population: 10,330,000
Capital: Prague
Official language: Czech
Currency: Koruna

◆ **Slovakia**
Area: 49,035 sq km
Population: 5,400,000
Capital: Bratislava
Official language: Slovak
Currency: Koruna

◆ **Hungrary**
Area: 93,034 sq km
Population: 10,294,000
Capital: Budapest
Official language: Hungarian
Currency: Forint

◆ **Latvia**
Area: 63,700 sq km
Population: 2,700,000
Capital: Riga
Official language: Latvian
Currency: Lats

◆ **Lithuania**
Area: 65,200 sq km
Population: 3,742,000
Capital: Kiev
Official language: Vilnius
Currency: Litas

◆ **Estonia**
Area: 45,100 sq km
Population: 1,517,000
Capital: Tallinn
Official language: Estonian
Currency: Kroon—

Historical Prague
Prague, capital of the Czech Republic, is a fine old city on the River Vltava. Prague was the chief city of independent Bohemia in the Middle Ages.

The last of the bisons
The European bison, also known as the wisent, was resued from the brink of extinction in the 1950s and can be seen today in Poland's Bialowieza forest, on the Belarussian border.

Catholic Lithuania
St. Anne's Church and the Church of the Bernardines are in Vilnius, the Lithuanian capital. Like neighbouring Poland, Lithuania is a strongly Roman Catholic country.

The zither
This stringed instrument has a metallic sound which is popular in the folk music of Hungary and neighbouring countries.

Sounds of the balalaika
The balalaika is a musical instrument with a triangular body and a long neck like a guitar. Its jangling sounds are popular in Central Europe, Russia and the Balkans.

BALKANS AND ROMANIA

THE STATES OF SOUTHERN Central Europe are known as the Balkans. They take their name from the Balkan peninsula, a great wedge of land which stretches south into the Mediterranean.

The warm, blue waters around the Balkan coast form the Adriatic, Aegean and Black Seas and are popular with tourists. The region is mountainous, with hot, dry summers. Winters are severe in the north of the region, but generally mild in the south. Earthquakes are common. The Balkan countries produce fruit, wines and spirits, dairy products such as yoghurt and cheese, olives, sunflowers and tobacco.

In the early 1990s the northwest of the region saw bitter fighting as the large nation of Yugoslavia broke up into separate independent states. These took the names of **Slovenia**, **Croatia**, **Bosnia-Herzegovina**, **Yugoslavia** (Serbia and Montenegro), and **Macedonia** (which is also the name of the northernmost province of Greece). The small and very poor country of **Albania** also suffered from political unrest and civil war in the 1990s.

The northeast of the Balkan peninsula is occupied by **Bulgaria**, a land of fertile farmland to the south of the river Danube, crossed by the Balkan and Rhodope mountain chains. Its northern neighbour is **Romania**, lying around the forested Carpathian mountain range and the Transylvanian Alps. On the Black Sea coast, the river Danube forms a marshy delta region.

The Balkan peninsula narrows to the south, breaking up into the headland of the Peloponnese and scattered island chains. **Greece** was the centre of Europe's first great civilizations, between 4,000 and 2,000 years ago. The rock of the Acropolis, with its temple, the Parthenon, still towers above the Greek capital, Athens.

Off to market

Romanian farmers gather for a cattle fair at Sugatag. The population as a whole is made up of Romanians, whose language is linked to the Latin language of the ancient Roman empire, as well as Magyars and Gypsies.

The sunflower crop

Sunflowers are grown in many parts of southern Europe. Their seeds may be roasted and eaten as snacks, turned into cooking oil or used to make margarine.

Old-fashioned style

Traditional Bulgarian costumes, with waistcoats, aprons and skirts may still be seen at many festivals or folk dances.

Fact Box

◆ **Slovenia**
Area: 20,250 sq km
Population: 1,990,000
Capital: Ljublana
Official language: Slovenian
Currency: Tolar

◆ **Croatia**
Area: 56,540 sq km
Population: 4,789,000
Capital: Zagreb
Official language: Serbo-Croat
Currency: Croatian dinar

◆ **Bosnia-Herzegovina**
Area: 51,130 sq km
Population: 4,366,000
Capital: Sarajevo
Official language: Serbo-Croat
Currency: Bosnian dinar

◆ **Yugoslavia (Serbia-Montenegro)**
Area: 102,170 sq km
Population: 10,600,000
Capital: Belgrade
Official language: Serbo-Croat
Currency: Dinar

◆ **Macedonian (former Yugoslav) Republic**
Area: 25,715 sq km
Population: 2,173,000
Capital: Skopje
Official language: Macedonian
Currency: Dinar

◆ **Albania**
Area: 28,750 sq km
Population: 3,363,000
Capital: Tiranë
Official language: Albanian
Currency: Lek

◆ **Romania**
Area: 237,500 sq km
Population: 22,767,000
Capital: Bucharest
Official language: Romanian
Currency: Leu

◆ **Bulgaria**
Area: 110,900 sq km
Population: 8,469,000
Capital: Sofia
Official language: Bulgarian
Currency: Lev

◆ **Greece**
Area: 131,985 sq km
Population: 10,500,000
Capital: Athens
Official language: Greek
Currency: Drachma

Clear waters
A waterfall sparkles in the sunshine in Croatia. This is a small country of many landscapes.

Islands from volcanoes
The Greek island of Santorini (or Thira) is one of the islands that form the Cyclades in the Aegean Sea. Once a volcano, the island has steep cliffs and narrow, winding streets. It has become a popular destination for tourists.

RUSSIA AND ITS NEIGHBOURS

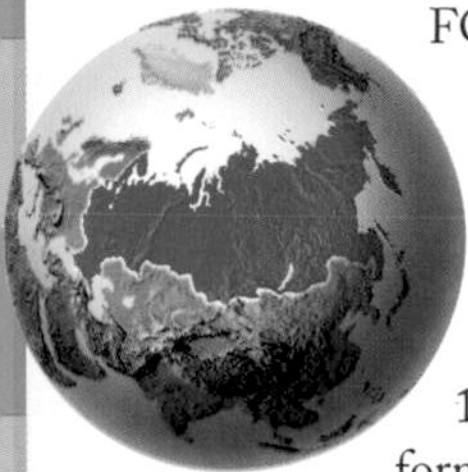

FOR A LARGE PART OF THIS CENTURY all the countries on this map were part of one huge country, the Soviet Union. That nation was formed in the years after November 1917, when communists seized power from the czars. Communist rule ended in 1991 and many of the regions around the former Soviet borders then broke away to become independent countries.

St Basil's Cathedral, Russia
Moscow is famous for the onion-shaped domes of St Basil's Cathedral. It was built in 1555 by Czar Ivan IV to commemorate the defeat of invading Tartars.

The remaining part of the former Soviet Union was renamed the '**Russian Federation**'. It is still by far the largest country in the world, stretching across two continents, Europe and Asia. Eighty percent of the population are Russians, but the rest belong to one of the many other ethnic groups who live in this enormous region.

Northern Russia is a land of tundra, where deep-frozen soil borders the Arctic Ocean. To the south is the great belt of forest known as taiga, whose spruce trees are heavy with snow during the long, bitter winter. Southern Russia and the **Ukraine** have the fertile black earth of the rolling grasslands known as steppes. The lands to the south of Russia's new borders take in warm, fertile valleys, thin grasslands grazed by sheep and goats, deserts and high mountains.

Russia is rich in minerals, oil, natural gas and timber. Its industries were developed in a hurry during the Soviet years, but at great cost to its people and environment. Russia is still an economic giant, producing machinery, textiles, chemicals and vehicles.

Happy Easter!
Many Russians are Christians belonging to the Eastern Orthodox Church. Traditionally, they exchanged beautifully decorated eggs as gifts at Easter.

Coarse cotton
Cotton of a tough, coarse grade is grown in Uzbekistan. The country is a major world producer, but in this dry land the cotton crop needs a great deal of irrigation, and this has harmed the environment.

FACT BOX

◆ **Russia**
Area: 17,078,005 sq km
Population: 148,673,000
Capital: Moscow
Official language: Russian
Currency: Rouble

◆ **Belarus**
Area: 208,000 sq km
Population: 10,313,000
Capital: Minsk
Official language: Belarussian
Currency: Rouble

◆ **Ukraine**
Area: 603,700 sq km
Population: 52,194,000
Capital: Kiev
Official language: Ukrainian
Currency: Karbovanets

◆ **Moldova**
Area: 33,7000 sq km
Population: 4,356,000
Capital: Chisinau
Official language: Moldovan
Currency: Leu

◆ **Kazakhstan**
Area: 2,717,300 sq km
Population: 17,035,000
Capital: Almaty
Official language: Kazakh
Currency: Tenge

◆ **Armenia**
Area: 30,000 sq km
Population: 3,677,000
Capital: Yerevan
Official language: Armenian
Currencies: Dram, rouble

◆ **Georgia**
Area: 69,700 sq km
Population: 5,471,000
Capital: Tbilisi
Official language: Georgian
Currency: Lari

◆ **Azerbaijan**
Area: 87,000 sq km
Population: 7,398,000
Capital: Baku
Official language: Azeri
Currencies: Manat, rouble

◆ **Turkmenistan**
Area: 488,100 sq km
Population: 3,714,000
Capital: Ashkhabad
Official language: Turkmen
Currency: Manat

◆ **Uzbekistan**
Area: 447,400 sq km
Population: 21,207,000
Capital: Tashkent
Official language: Uzbek
Currencies: Som, rouble

◆ **Tajikstan**
Area: 143,100 sq km
Population: 5,514,000
Capital: Dushanbe
Official language: Tajik
Currency: Rouble

◆ **Kyrgyzstan**
Area: 198,500 sq km
Population: 4,528,000
Capital: Bishkek
Official language: Kyrgyz
Currency: Som

In the Caucasus
This woman wears a traditional costume of Dagostan, a part of the Russian Federation which lies between the Caucasus mountains and the Caspian Sea. About 30 different ethnic groups live in this region.

CANADA AND GREENLAND

FACT BOX

◆ **Canada**
Area: 9,922,385 sq km
Population: 30,000,000
Capital: Ottawa
Official languages: French, English

◆ **Greenland**
Area: 2,175,600 sq km
Population: 57,000
Capital: Nuuk (Godthåb)
Official languages: Danish, Inuktitut
Currency: Danish krone

CANADA is the second largest country in the world and yet it is home to only 30 million people. Most Canadians live in the big cities in the south, such as Toronto, Ottawa, Montréal and Vancouver.

The southern provinces take in the St Lawrence River and Seaway, the Great Lakes, the prairies along the United States border and the foggy coasts of the Atlantic and Pacific Oceans.

The severe climate makes it hard for people to live in the northern wilderness, which stretches into the **Arctic Circle**. Here, a broad belt of spruce forest gives way to bare, deep-frozen soil called tundra, and a maze of islands locked in ice.

Canada's wilderness includes rivers, lakes, coasts and forests. It is home to polar bears and seals, caribou, moose, beavers and loons. It also has valuable resources, providing timber, hydroelectric power and minerals, including oil. **Canada** is a wealthy country.

The first Canadians crossed into North America from Asia long ago, when the two continents were joined by land. They were the Native American peoples and they were followed by the Inuit people of the Arctic. Today these two groups make up only four percent of the population. About 40 percent of Canadians are descended from peoples of the British Isles, especially Scots. People of French descent make up 27 percent, and there are also many people of Eastern European and Asian descent.

Canada has two official languages, French and English. In recent years many people in the French-speaking province of Québec have campaigned to become separate from the rest of Canada.

Across the Davis Strait, **Greenland** (or Kallaalit Nunaat) is a self-governing territory of Denmark. Its peoples are descended from both Inuit and Scandinavians.

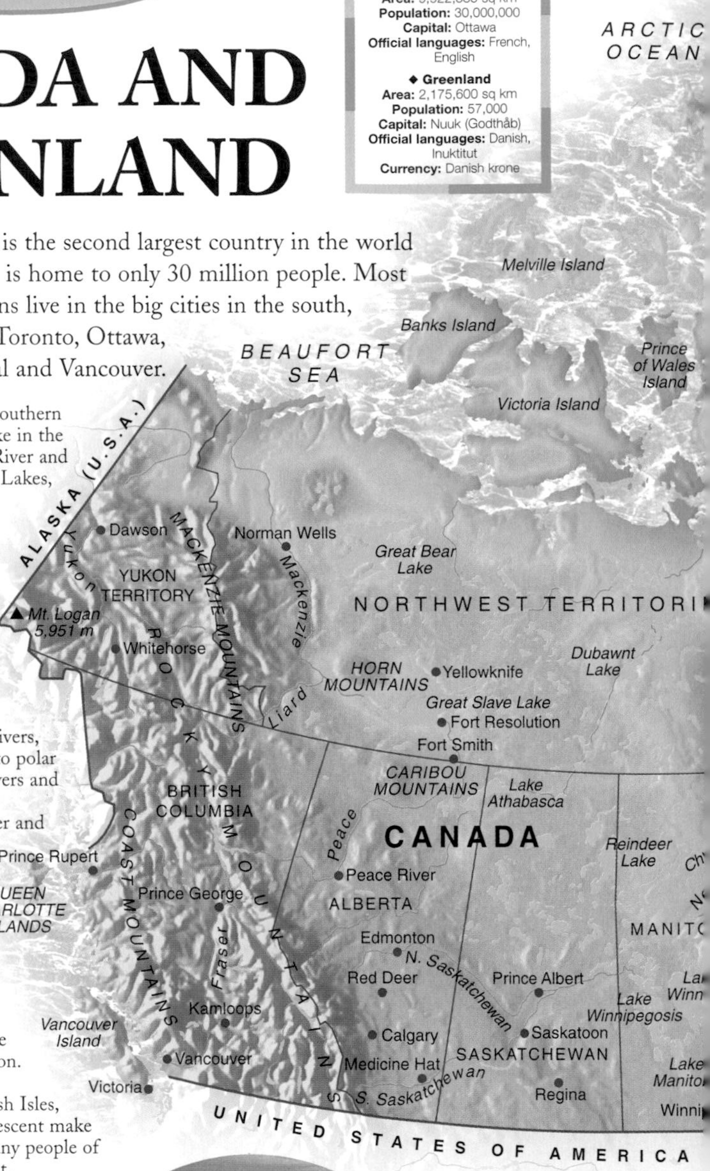

Wheat Harvest
Large combine harvesters cross the Canadian prairies. These are natural grasslands which are now largely given over to wheat and cattle production. They occupy parts of Manitoba, Saskatchewan and Alberta and stretch across the border into the northern United States.

Toronto, Ontario view over city
The CN Tower soars 553 metres above Canada's largest city, Toronto. This is a centre of business and industry built on the shores of Lake Ontario. It is also the capital of the vast province of Ontario.

Arctic travel
In the ice and snow of the Canadian Arctic and Greenland, travelling can be difficult. Snowmobiles, rather like motorcycles with skis instead of wheels, have now mostly replaced the traditional dog sleds.

Ice hockey
Fast and hard, ice hockey is one of Canada's most popular spectator sports. The game was invented in Canada, its rules being drawn up in Montréal in 1879. There are two teams of six skaters. Both Canadian and US teams compete within two major leagues.

North America

USA

THE UNITED STATES OF AMERICA

make up a huge country, which crosses no less than eight time zones. It extends from the Pacific to the Atlantic Oceans, from Canada south to Mexico.

The modern nation was formed by colonists from Europe, who from the 1500s onwards seized and settled the lands of the Native American peoples. In 1776 the British colonies in the east declared their independence, and the new country grew rapidly during the 1800s as it gained territory from France, Mexico and Russia. Today, in addition to the small Native American population, there are Americans whose ancestors originally came from Britain, Ireland, Italy, France, Germany, the Netherlands and Poland. There are African Americans, whose ancestors were brought to America to work as slaves. There are Armenians, Spanish, Chinese, Cubans, Vietnamese and Koreans. All are citizens of the United States.

The nation today is a federation of 50 states, which have the power to pass many of their own laws. The federal capital is at Washington, a large city on the Potomac River, in the District of Columbia (DC). Here is the Congress, made up of a Senate and a House of Representatives, and the White House, the home of the US presidents.

The American economy is the most powerful in the world. The country is rich in minerals, including oil, coal and iron ore. American companies produce computers and software, aircraft, cars and processed foods. There are also many large banks and finance companies. America leads in space exploration and technology. The films and television programmes produced in America are watched by people in many countries around the world.

The woods of Vermont
Vermont is in New England and nicknamed the Green Mountain State. It is famous for its brilliant foliage in the autumn or fall.

Fact Box

◆ **United States of America**
Area: 9,363,130 sq km
Population: 267,700,000
Capital: Washington DC
Official language: English
Currency: US dollar

Monument Valley, Arizona

This spectacular landscape is sculpted by nature and is formed of red sandstone. There are many Wild West legends rooted here.

The Bald Eagle

This is America's national bird. It has a white head, and a wingspan of up to 2 metres. Its natural habitat is by lakes and rivers, and for food it preys mainly on fish and rodents.

The northeastern United States have a mild climate, although winter snowfall can be heavy and summers can be warm. Inland from the rocks and stormy shores of the Atlantic coast are the woodlands of the New England region, which turn to every shade of red and gold in the autumn. Here there are broad rivers and neat little towns dating back to the days of the early settlers, as well as the historic city of Boston, Massachusetts. In the far north the Great Lakes mark the border with Canada. On this border are the spectacular Niagara Falls, a major tourist attraction which also provides valuable hydroelectric power. The Appalachian mountain ranges run for 2,400 kilometres from north to south, through the eastern United States.

The northeastern United States include centres of industry and mining, and large cities with gleaming skyscrapers, sprawling suburbs, road and rail networks. New York City, centred around the island of Manhattan, is the business capital of the United States and also a lively centre of arts and entertainment. To many people, New York City is a symbol of America – fast-moving and energetic, a melting pot of different peoples and cultures. The northern city of Detroit is a centre of the motor industry, and Chicago, on the windy shores of Lake Michigan, is another bustling city of skyscrapers, and an important centre of business and manufacture.

Travelling south from the Delaware River and the great city of Philadelphia, you come to the federal District of Columbia, the site of Washington, capital city of the United States. Approaching the American South, you pass into warmer country where tobacco and cotton are grown in the red earth. The long peninsula of Florida extends southwards into the Caribbean Sea, fringed by sandy islands called keys. Along the Gulf coast the climate is hot and very humid, with creeks known as bayous and tangled swamps which are home to alligators.

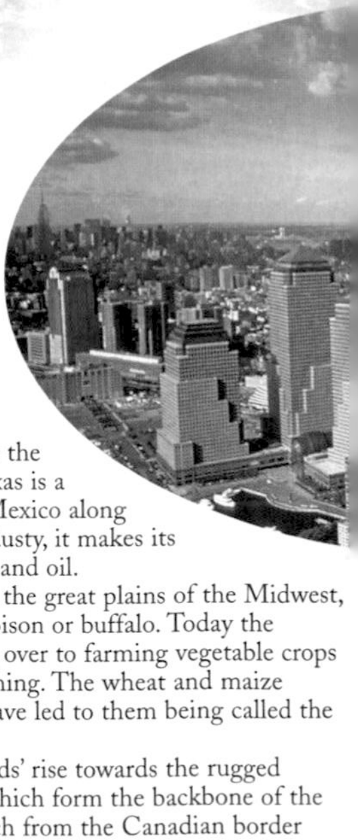

Hurricanes are common in late summer and autumn. New Orleans, the home of jazz, has many picturesque old buildings with wrought-iron verandas. It lies 170 kilometres above the mouth of the Mississippi River, which together with the mighty Missouri drains the centre of the continent. Texas is a huge state which borders Mexico along the Rio Grande. Dry and dusty, it makes its living from cattle ranching and oil.

Prairies once covered the great plains of the Midwest, the home of vast herds of bison or buffalo. Today the grasslands are largely given over to farming vegetable crops and grain, or to cattle ranching. The wheat and maize produced on the Prairies have led to them being called the 'breadbasket of the world'.

Barren, stony 'badlands' rise towards the rugged Rocky Mountain ranges, which form the backbone of the United States as they stretch from the Canadian border south to Mexico. Southwards and westwards again there are large areas of burning desert, salt flats and canyons, where over the ages the rocks have been worn into fantastic shapes by wind and water. In places the Grand Canyon of Arizona is 24 kilometres wide and two kilometres deep, a spectacular gorge cut out by the waters of the Colorado River.

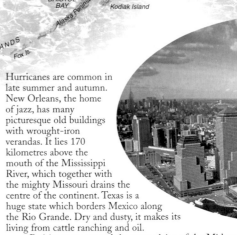

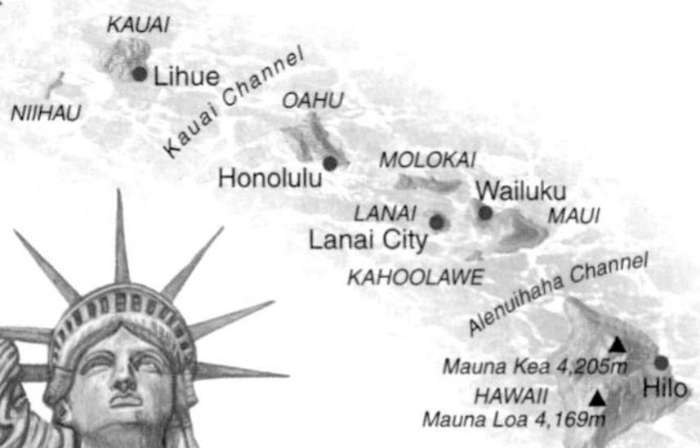

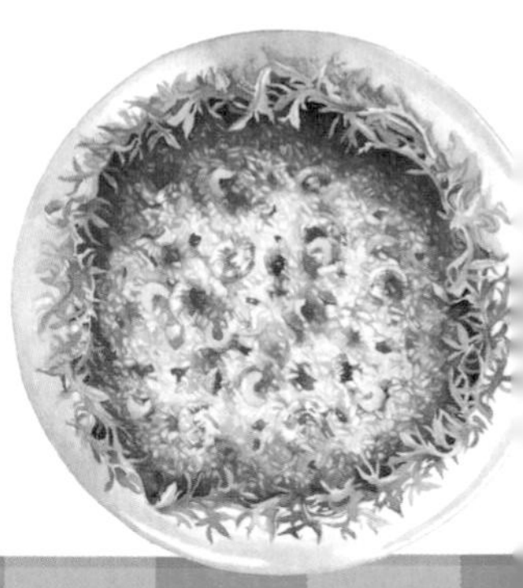

Jambalaya!

Rice, seafood, green peppers and hot spices make up this delicious dish from New Orleans, in Louisiana. The people of this city include many of French and African descent, and this shows in its cooking.

The Statue of Liberty

This huge monument, a gift from the people of France in 1886, was the first sight of America for many immigrants.

Badwater, in California's harsh Death Valley, is the lowest point in the United States, 86 metres below sea level.

The Sierra, Cascade and Coast ranges run parallel with the beautiful Pacific coast. The warm beaches, pines and gigantic redwood trees of California stretch northwards to the ferny forests of Oregon and Washington State, which is rainy and cool. Irrigation has made it possible to farm large areas of California, which produce citrus fruits and grape vines. Major cities of the west include Los Angeles, which takes in the world-famous film studios of Hollywood, beautiful San Francisco, set on a wide bay which can be warm and sparkling blue or shrouded in cool sea-fog, and the busy northern port of Seattle.

The United States has a northern outpost in oil-rich Alaska, its largest state. Alaska was purchased from Russia in 1867. Bordered by Canada, the Alaskan wilderness stretches into the remote Arctic, a deep frozen land of mountains and tundra. Its islands are inhabited by large grizzly bears and its waters by schools of migrating whales. Mount McKinley, at 6,194 metres, is the highest point not just in the United States, but in all of North America.

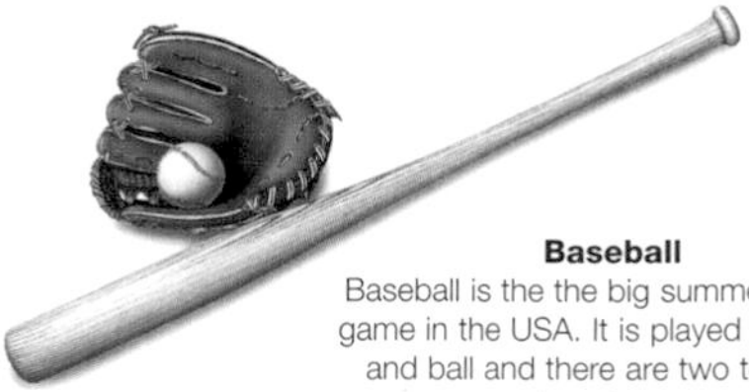

Baseball
Baseball is the the big summer-season game in the USA. It is played with a bat and ball and there are two teams of nine players.

Far to the west, in the Pacific Ocean, the Hawaiian Islands are also part of the United States. Tourists come here to enjoy the warm climate and the surf and to see the islands' spectacular volcanoes.

The United States also governs or has special links with various other territories, such as American Samoa, the Northern Marianas and the Midway Islands in the Pacific Ocean. Puerto Rico and the US Virgin Islands in the Caribbean are also governed by the United States.

The United States has close economic links with its neighbours, Canada and Mexico, through the North American Free Trade Agreement of 1994. It is also a member of many other international groupings, such as the the North Atlantic Treaty Organization (NATO), a military alliance which links it with Western and Central Europe.

As the world's most powerful country, the influence of the United States is to be seen in many other lands. Films and television programmes have made the American way of life influential around the world. Hamburgers and soft drinks are now bought in many other countries. American blues and jazz has influenced all kinds of popular music and American slang is used by people around the world.

Manhattan
The centre of New York City is built over the island of Manhattan. Unable to build outwards, architects have built upwards. The skyline includes many famous skyscrapers. These twin towers belong to the World Trade Centre.

Cops and crime
American policemen and detectives fight city crime. Their work has been made famous around the world by countless films and television series.

Heart of the nation
The impressive Capitol building is at the centre of Washington, District of Columbia. It is used by the United States Congress and was constructed between 1851 and 1863.

Blast-off!
The space shuttle leaves Earth on another mission. The United States has been a pioneer of space exploration since the 1960s.

North America

Mexico, Central America & the Caribbean

Ancient stones
Many great civilizations developed in ancient times in Mexico and Central America. Statues like this, called chacmools, were used during human sacrifices.

MEXICO is a large, mountainous country with a tropical climate. It stretches southwards from the Rio Grande on the United States border, and meets the Pacific Ocean in the west and the Gulf of Mexico in the east.

Mexico is a land of deserts, forests and volcanoes, dotted with the spectacular ruins of ancient Native American civilizations, such as the Maya, Toltec and Aztec. Mexico City, built on the site of an ancient Aztec city, is a vast, sprawling centre of population.

To the south, **Central America** narrows to a thin strip of land called the isthmus of Panama. Guatemala, Belize, Honduras, El Salvador, Nicaragua, Costa Rica and Panama are all small nations that live mostly by farming tropical crops such as bananas, coffee and sugar-cane. Many Mexicans and Central Americans are of Native American, Spanish or mixed descent.

Birds of a feather
The quetzal is a brilliantly coloured bird. It lives in rainforests from southern Mexico to Panama, where it feeds on berries and fruits.

Many people in Mexico and Central America are poor and the region has a long history of political strife and civil war.

The **Caribbean Sea** is part of the Atlantic Ocean and is dotted with beautiful islands in warm, blue seas. These were once home to Native American peoples such as the Arawaks and the Caribs, after whom the region is named. Then came European invaders, including the Spanish, Dutch, French and British. Most of today's Caribbeans are descended from West Africans who were brought in as slaves by the early settlers. Caribbean islanders live by fishing, farming, manufacture and tourism. Favourite sports include baseball in Cuba and cricket in Jamaica and Barbados. The region is famous for its range of popular music, from calypso to salsa, from reggae to soca.

Coconut grove
Palms line sandy beaches in the Central American republic of Costa Rica. Coconuts are common around the tropical coasts of Central America and the Caribbean.

People of Panama
The Kuna are an indigenous people who live on the coasts and islands of Panama and Colombia. They mostly live by fishing and are well known for their craft work, which includes wood carving and the making of molas, the colourful blouses being worn here.

FACT BOX

◆ **Mexico**
Area: 1,972,545 sq km
Population: 95,700,000
Capital: Mexico City
Main language: Spanish
Currency: Mexican peso

◆ **Belize**
Area: 22,965 sq km
Population: 205,000
Capital: Belmopan
Main language: English
Currency: Belize dollar

◆ **Costa Rica**
Area: 50,900 sq km
Population: 3,500,000
Capital: San José
Main language: Spanish
Currency: Costa Rican colón

◆ **El Salvador**
Area: 21,395 sq km
Population: 5,900,000
Capital: San Salvador
Main language: Spanish
Currency: El Salvador colón

◆ **Guatemala**
Area: 108,890 sq km
Population: 11,200,000
Capital: Guatemala City
Main language: Spanish
Currency: Quetzal

◆ **Honduras**
Area: 112,085 sq km
Population: 5,800,000
Capital: Tegucigalpa
Main language: Spanish
Currency: Lempira

◆ **Nicaragua**
Area: 148,000 sq km
Population: 4,400,000
Capital: Managua
Main language: Spanish
Currency: Córdoba

◆ **Panama**
Area: 78,515 sq km
Population: 2,700,000
Capital: Panama City
Main language: Spanish
Currency: Balboa

◆ **Antigua and Barbuda**
Area: 442 sq km
Population: 100,000
Capital: St Johns
Main language: English
Currency: East Caribbean dollar

◆ **Bahamas**
Area: 13,865 sq km
Population: 300,000
Capital: Nassau
Main language: English
Currency: Bahamian dollar

◆ **Barbados**
Area: 430 sq km
Population: 300,000
Capital: Bridgetown
Main language: English
Currency: Barbados dollar

◆ **Cuba**
Area: 114,525 sq km
Population: 11,100,000
Capital: Havana
Main language: Spanish
Currency: Cuban peso

◆ **Dominica**
Area: 751 sq km
Population: 100,000
Capital: Roseau
Main language: English
Currency: East Caribbean dollar

◆ **Dominican Republic**
Area: 48,440 sq km
Population: 8,200,000
Capital: Santiago
Main language: Spanish
Currency: Peso

◆ **Grenada**
Area: 345 sq km
Population: 100,000
Capital: St George's
Main language: English
Currency: East Caribbean dollar

◆ **Haiti**
Area: 27,750 sq km
Population: 6,600,000
Capital: Port-au-Prince
Main language: French
Currency: Gourde

◆ **Jamaica**
Area: 11,425 sq km
Population: 2,600,000
Capital: Kingston
Main language: English
Currency: Jamaican dollar

◆ **St Christoper (St Kitts) – Nevis**
Area: 261 sq km
Population: 44,000
Capital: Basseterre
Main language: English
Currency: East Caribbean dollar

◆ **St Lucia**
Area: 616 sq km
Population: 139,000
Capital: Castries
Main language: English
Currency: East Caribbean dollar

◆ **St Vincent and the Grenadines**
Area: 389 sq km
Population: 111,000
Capital: Kingstown
Main language: English
Currency: East Caribbean dollar

◆ **Trinidad and Tobago**
Area: 5,130 sq km
Population: 1,300,000
Capital: Port of Spain
Main language: English
Currency: Trinidad & Tobago dollar

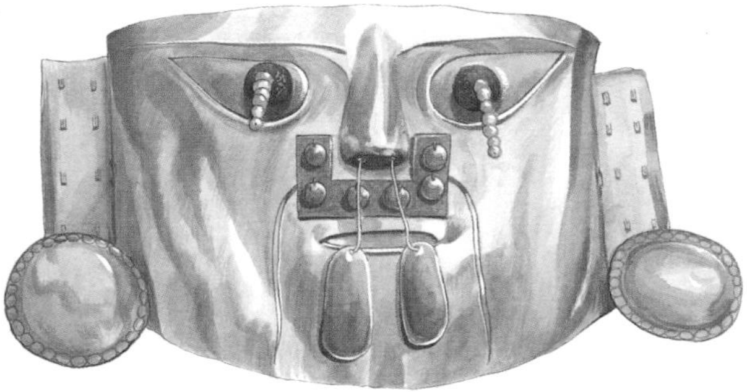

Inca crafts
This mask was made by Inca goldsmiths in Peru. The Incas came to power in the 1400s and were famous for their beautiful work with gold.

SOUTH AMERICA

NORTHERN ANDEAN COUNTRIES

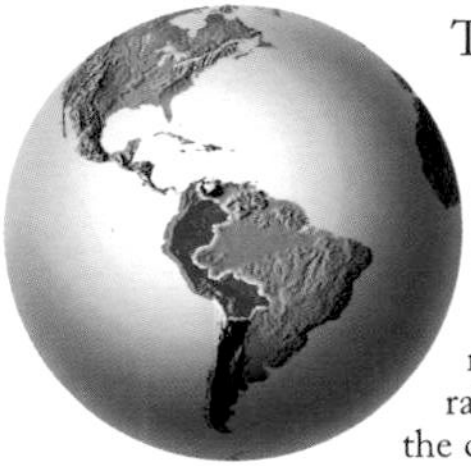

THE ANDES MOUNTAINS extend down the whole length of South America, from north to south. They rise in Colombia, the country which borders the narrow land link with Central America, the Isthmus of Panama.

Colombia is a beautiful country with three ranges of the Andes running through it. The mountains slope east to grasslands and then to rainforest. The chief cities are on the coast, which is warm and humid, or in the cooler mountain regions. The mountains are mined for gold, emeralds, salt and coal.

The Andes rise to 6,267 metres above sea level at Chimborazo in **Ecuador**. Bananas and sugar-cane are grown here. In the cooler foothills of the Andes coffee is an important crop. To the east of the mountains are rainforests, where oil is drilled. Ecuador is the second largest oil producer in South America after Venezuela.

In the 1400s, **Peru** was the centre of the mighty Inca empire an advanced Native American civilization produced beautiful textiles and jewellery in gold and precious stones. Ruined Inca cities such as Machu Picchu still perch high amongst the peaks of the Andes. Terraced hillsides allow crops such as potatoes to be grown in the mountains. Fishing is important along the foggy Pacific coast. In the far east, rivers flow through tropical forests into the river Amazon.

Lake Titicaca lies high in the Andes on the border between Peru and **Bolivia**. Bolivia is an inland country which lies across the high plateau of the Altiplano, where most Bolivians live, and stretches into hot, humid rainforest in the east. The city of La Paz is the world's highest capital city, at 3,660 metres above sea level. Bolivia produces tin, timber, rubber and potatoes.

The lands of the northern Andes are home to many Native Americans, such as the Quechua and Aymara peoples. The whole region was ruled by Spain from the 1500s to the

Fact Box

◆ **Colombia**
Area: 1,138,915 sq km
Population: 37,400,000
Capital: Bogotá
Main language: Spanish
Currency: Colombian peso

◆ **Ecuador**
Area: 461,475 sq km
Population: 12,000,000
Capital: Quito
Main language: Spanish
Currency: Sucre

◆ **Bolivia**
Area: 1,098,580 sq km
Population: 7,800,000
Capitals: La Paz, Sucre
Main language: Spanish
Currency: Boliviano

◆ **Peru**
Area: 1,285,215 sq km
Population: 24,400,000
Capital: Lima
Main language: Spanish
Currency: Nuevo soll

Lake Titicaca
This lake lies on the mountainous border between Bolivia and Peru. At 3810 metres above sea level, this is the world's highest navigable lake.

Pan pipes
Sounds of the Andes include haunting folk tunes accompanied by panpipes, drums and various types of guitar. They have been influenced by Native American and Spanish music.

Machu Picchu, Inca ruins
High in the Peruvian Andes stand the ruins of this Inca city, Machu Picchu. The city was never found by the Spanish conquerors of Peru and it remained undiscovered until 1911.

The incredible llama
The llama is a sure-footed but stubborn member of the camel family. It is used to carry goods over the high passes of the Andes mountains.

Coffee beans
Brazil is the world's biggest producer of coffee. The crop is mostly grown in the south, on large estates and is exported worldwide.

Rio panorama
A huge statue of Christ stands high above the Brazilian port of Rio de Janeiro.

BRAZIL AND ITS NEIGHBOURS

Rainforest creatures
The vast forests which are drained by the River Amazon, support all kinds of wildlife, such as this brightly coloured macaw. Sadly, many species are threatened by the clearance of the forests by farmers and illegal traders in wildlife.

BRAZIL is South America's largest nation. It includes grasslands, fertile plateaus and dry areas of scrub.

About a third of the country is taken up by tropical rainforests. All kinds of rare plants, parrots, snakes and monkeys live in these dense, dripping forests, which are under threat from road-builders, farmers, miners and loggers. The forests are crossed by hundreds of rivers, which drain into the wide, muddy waters of the Amazon, one of the world's two longest rivers. The river basin of the Amazon is the world's largest, covering 7,045,000 square kilometres.

Most Brazilians live in the big cities of the Atlantic coast, such as Rio de Janeiro and São Paolo. The country has rich resources, but many of the population are poor people who live in shacks built on the outskirts of the city. Brasília, with its broad avenues and high-rise buildings, was specially built as the country's new capital city in the 1960s.

To the northeast of Brazil, on the Caribbean coast, is **Venezuela**. This land, crossed by the Orinoco River, includes rainforests, high mountains and the tropical grassy plains of the Llanos. The beautiful Angel Falls (the world's highest at 979 metres) provide hydroelectric power, while Lake Maracaibo, in the northwest, is rich in oil.

The three other countries on the Caribbean coast are **Guyana**, **Surinam** and **French Guiana**. The first was once a British colony, the second was a Dutch colony and the third is still an overseas department governed by France. Most people live in the humid regions of the coast, while the rainforests and mountains of the remote south are more sparsely populated. Crops include sugar-cane, coffee, rice and bananas. An important mineral is bauxite, used in the making of aluminium.

Many different ethnic groups live in the region as a whole, including Native American peoples who have had to struggle to survive ever since Europeans invaded the region in the 1500s. The population of northern South America also includes many people of Asian, African, European and mixed descent, with ancestors from Spain, Portugal, Italy, Germany, France, Netherlands and Britain.

Fishing for a living
A fishing crew check their tackle as children play on the beach. This scene is near Salvador, capital of the tropical Bahía region in northeastern Brazil.

FACT BOX

◆ **Brazil**
Area: 8,511,965 sq km
Population: 160,300,000
Capital: Brasília
Main language: Portuguese
Currency: Cruzeiro real

◆ **Venezuela**
Area: 912,045 sq km
Population: 22,600,000
Capital: Caracas
Main language: Spanish
Currency: Bolívar

◆ **Guyana**
Area: 214,970 sq km
Population: 800,000
Capital: Georgetown
Main language: English
Currency: Guyana dollar

◆ **Surinam**
Area: 163,820 sq km
Population: 446,000
Capital: Paramaribo
Official language: Dutch
Currency: Surinam guilder

◆ **French Guiana**
Area: 91,000 sq km
Population: 300,000
Capital: Cayenne
Main language: French
Currency: French franc

Yanomami hunters
About 13,000 Yanomami people live in Venezuela and another 8000 in Brazil. They live by hunting, fishing and growing food in the rainforest.

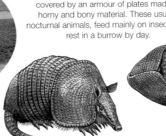

Paraná River, Paraguay
Separating Paraguay and Argentina the Parana River flows some 4,500 km. The English explorer Sebastian Cabot was the first to sail up it in 1526.

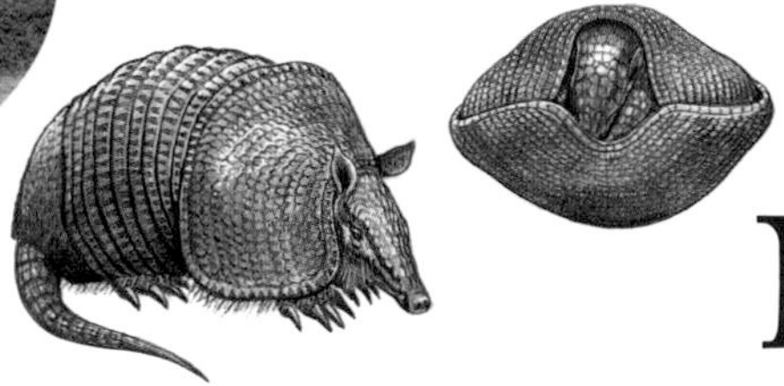

Armadillo
The head and body of the armadillo is covered by an armour of plates made of horny and bony material. These usually nocturnal animals, feed mainly on insects and rest in a burrow by day.

ARGENTINA AND ITS NEIGHBOURS

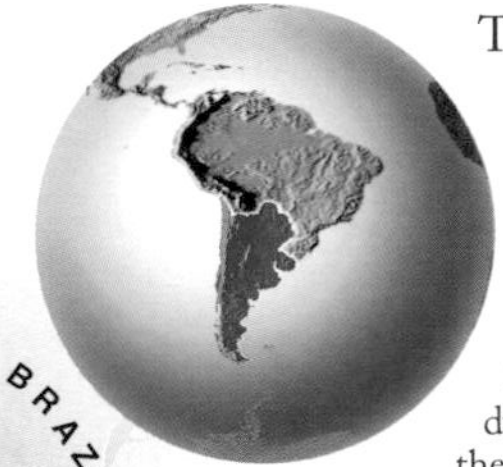

THE SOUTHERN PART of South America stretches from the hot and humid Gran Chaco region to the cold and stormy waters of Tierra del Fuego and Cape Horn.

The largest country of this region is **Argentina**. Its highly populated capital is Buenos Aires on the river Plate. More than eight out of every ten Argentineans are city dwellers. However it was the country's cattle-farming regions – the Pampa grasslands and the northeast – that in the last 150 years brought wealth to the country and attracted large numbers of settlers from Europe. Argentina's western borders follow the high peak of the Andes range, which reach their highest point at Cerro Aconcagua (6,959 metres above sea level). To the south are the windswept plateaus of Patagonia, largely given over to sheep farming. The port of Ushuaia is the southernmost town in the world.

Northwards from Buenos Aires, across the river Plate, lies Montevideo, capital of **Uruguay**. This is another country which raises cattle and sheep, and whose rich grasslands and mild climate attracted European settlers. Neighbouring **Paraguay** is far from the coast. Most of its people farm the hills and plains of the east. Few live in the hot wilderness of the Gran Chaco.

To the west of the Andes is **Chile**, which covers a long and narrow area. Here is one of the driest regions on Earth, the Atacama desert. It also includes fertile orchards and productive vineyards, the big city of Santiago and the spectacular glaciers of the southern Andes. Spanish is spoken throughout the region, and some Native American languages such as Guaraní may also be heard.

URUGUAY

ARGENTINA

Buenos Aires by night
The Monument of the Two Congresses stands in front of the domed Palace of Congress, built in 1906. The Argentinian capital is a large, lively city.

Fact Box

◆ **Argentina**
Area: 2,780,090 sq km
Population: 35,600,000
Capital: Buenos Aires
Official language: Spanish
Currency: Peso

◆ **Chile**
Area: 736,000 sq km
Population: 14,600,000
Capital: Santiago
Official language: Spanish
Currency: Peso

◆ **Paraguay**
Area: 406,750 sq km
Population: 5,100,000
Capital: Asunción
Official language: Spanish
Currency: Guarani

◆ **Uruguay**
Area: 176,210 sq km
Population: 3,200,000
Capital: Montevideo
Official language: Spanish
Currency: Peso

Mountains, Southern Chile
The long, narrow country of Chile has vast differences in climate. There is hot desert in the north, Mediterranean type in the centre and cool, humid conditions in the south. Some mountains are permanently snow-capped.

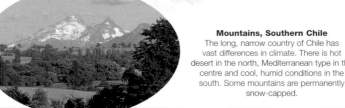

Prickly Pear
The flesh and seeds of the peeled fruit of the prickly pear have a pleasant taste. This cactus is low-growing and has flat oval stem joints and bright yellow flowers and occurs in Central and South America.

Turkish women
These women are from the port of Kas in southern Turkey. They are kneading dough and making pastry. Many Muslim women cover their heads with scarves or full veils.

SOUTHWEST ASIA

SOUTHWEST ASIA IS SOMETIMES described as the Near East or the Middle East. Its peoples include Greek Cypriots, Turks, Jews, Arabs, Kurds and Iranians.

The region has seen many political disputes and wars in recent years – between Greeks and Turks on Cyprus, between Palestinian Arabs and Jews in Israel, between Iraqi and Iranians and between Iraqui and Kuwaiti Arabs. The Kurds, whose homeland is occupied by **Iraq**, **Iran** and **Turkey**, have also been at the centre of conflict.

It was in Southwest Asia that the world's first civilizations grew up, between the rivers Tigris and Euphrates, over 6,000 years ago. The region later gave birth to three world faiths – Judaism, Christianity and Islam. In the days of the Roman empire the Jews were scattered from their homeland, and over the centuries their culture spread to Spain, Central and Eastern Europe and the Americas. Arab armies and traders took the Islamic faith into Africa and Spain, and Arab scholars made great advances in mathematics and astronomy. From the 1500s the Turks established a great empire which stretched from Central Europe to the Indian Ocean.

Southwest Asia includes vast deserts, in the Arabian peninsula and in eastern Iran. It also takes in fertile plains, the marshes of southern Iraq and mountain ranges of Turkey and Iran. The north of the region borders the Black Sea and the Caspian Sea, grassy steppes and the Caucasus mountains. To the east lies Afghanistan, Pakistan and the Indian sub-continent.

The region's most valuable resource is oil, which brings wealth to the governments of the lands around the Persian Gulf. However many ordinary people of Southwest Asia remain poor, living by herding goats, sheep or camels. In Israel and some other regions irrigation has made it possible to grow crops in harsh, dry environments. Oranges, dates, grapes and many kinds of nuts are grown in the region.

A summons to prayer
Mosques, like this one in Kuwait, have tall towers called minarets. From here, faithful Muslims are called to prayer. This message is often broadcast from loudspeakers. Muslims are expected to pray five times a day.

Wealth from oil
These supertankers are taking oil on board, off the coast of Saudi Arabia. Wealth from oil has transformed the economy of the Middle East and given great power to the many small countries around the Persian Gulf.

On the move
In many parts of Southwest Asia people live as nomads, wandering with their herds from one pasture to another, or following ancient trade routes.

Fact Box

◆ **Cyprus**
Area: 9,250 sq km
Population: 725,000
Capital: Nicosia
Official languages: Greek, Turkish
Currency: Cyprus pound

◆ **Lebanon**
Area: 10,400 sq km
Population: 3,900,000
Capital: Beirut
Official language: Arabic
Currency: Lebanese pound

◆ **Israel**
Area: 20,770 sq km
Population: 5,800,000
Capital: Jerusalem
Official languages: Hebrew, Arabic
Currency: Shekel

◆ **Jordan**
Area: 96,000 sq km
Population: 4,400,000
Capital: Amman
Official language: Arabic
Currency: Jordanian dinar

◆ **Syria**
Area: 185,680 sq km
Population: 15,000,000
Capital: Damascus
Official language: Arabic
Currency: Syrian pound

◆ **Turkey**
Area: 779,450 sq km
Population: 63,700,000
Capital: Ankara
Official language: Turkish
Currency: Turkish lira

◆ **Iraq**
Area: 438,445 sq km
Population: 21,2000,000
Capital: Baghdad
Official language: Arabic
Currency: Iraqi dinar

◆ **Iran**
Area: 1,648,000 sq km
Population: 67,500,000
Capital: Teheran
Official language: Farsi
Currency: Rial

◆ **United Arab Emirates**
Area: 75,150 sq km
Population: 2,300,000
Capital: Abu Dhabi
Official language: Arabic
Currency: Dirham

◆ **Qatar**
Area: 11,435 sq km
Population: 600,000
Capital: Doha
Official language: Arabic
Currency: Qatari rial

◆ **Oman**
Area: 271,950 sq km
Population: 2,300,000
Capital: Muscat
Official language: Arabic
Currency: Omani rial

◆ **Yemen**
Area: 527,970 sq km
Population: 15,200,000
Capital: San'a
Official language: Arabic
Currencies: Yemeni riyal, dinar

◆ **Saudi Arabia**
Area: 2,400,900 sq km
Population: 19,500,000
Capital: Riyadh
Official language: Arabic
Currency: Saudi riyal

◆ **Kuwait**
Area: 24,280 sq km
Population: 1,800,000
Capital: Kuwait City
Official language: Arabic
Currency: Kuwaiti dinar

◆ **Bahrain**
Area: 661 sq km
Population: 600,000
Capital: Manamah
Official language: Arabic
Currency: Bahraini dinar

Himalayan peaks
Breathtaking Mount Makalu, on the border between Nepal and China, rises to 8,470 metres above sea level. Eighty-eight percent of the world's mountains over 7,315 metres rise within the Himalaya-Karakoram ranges, many of them in the kingdom of Nepal.

INDIA AND ITS NEIGHBOURS

SOUTHERN ASIA stretches south into the Indian Ocean, forming a landmass so large that it sometimes called the 'sub-continent'. Its northern limits are marked by the Himalaya and Karakoram mountain ranges. These include many of the world's highest peaks and reach 8,848 metres above sea level at Everest, on Nepal's border with China.

The ranges pass through eastern Afghanistan, the Kashmir region on the border of India and Pakistan, India itself and the small mountain kingdoms of **Nepal** and **Bhutan**. Melting snows flow south from the mountains to form the five great rivers of the Punjab and also the mighty Ganges, which winds across the fertile plains of northern India before crossing Bangladesh into a maze of waterways around the Bay of Bengal. This area suffers from devastating floods.

Central and southern **India** form a triangular plateau called the Deccan, fringed on the east and west by the mountainous Ghats. These slopes are forested, catching the full force of the monsoon winds which bring rains from the Indian Ocean. For most of the year India is extremely hot and dry. Indian Ocean nations include the beautiful, tropical island of **Sri Lanka** and a chain of very low coral islands, the **Maldives**.

Advanced civilizations had developed around the river Indus by about 2500BC, and great religions grew up in India over the ages, including Hinduism, Buddhism and Sikhism. Invaders and traders brought Islam to the region. India today is a fascinating mixture of cultures, with over 800 different languages and dialects. There are many different customs, dress and foods. Spicy dishes from India are now popular everywhere.

The Indian sub-continent has a vast population, with many hungry mouths to feed. Many people make their living by farming, growing wheat, rice, millet, sugar-cane, coconut and tea. Most industries are based in the highly populated cities of India and Pakistan.

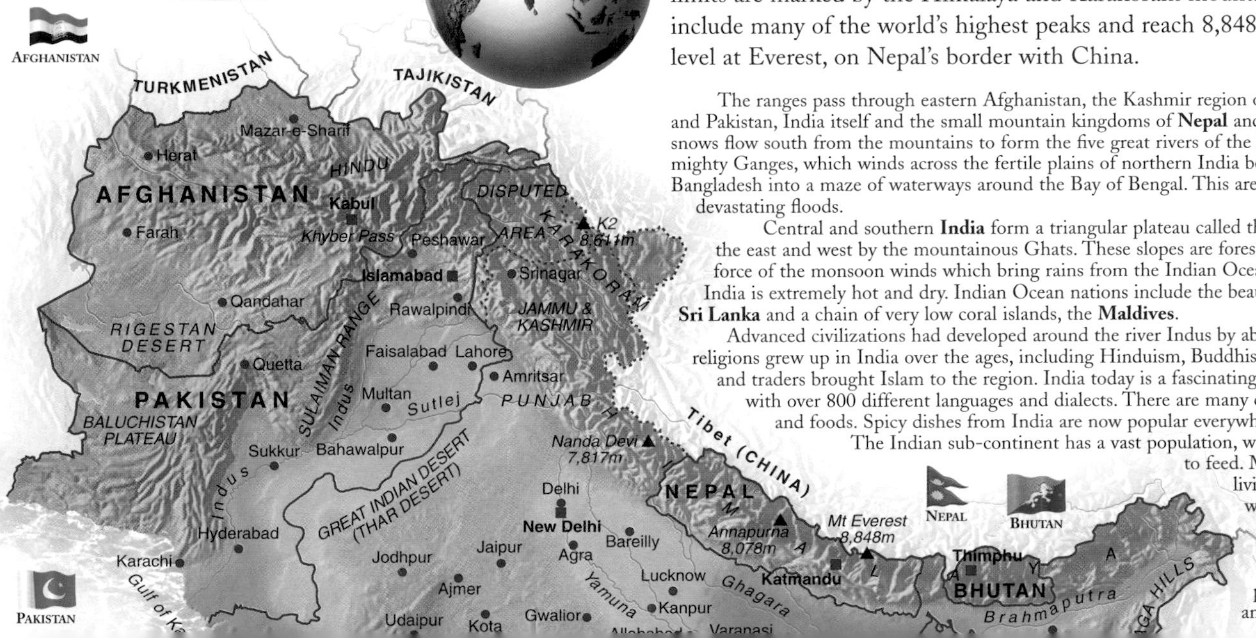

Tiger, tiger!

The fierce tiger is the biggest big cat, over 3 metres long. Its numbers have been greatly reduced by hunting and the cutting down of forests. Nepal, India and Bangladesh all protect the tiger in special reserves.

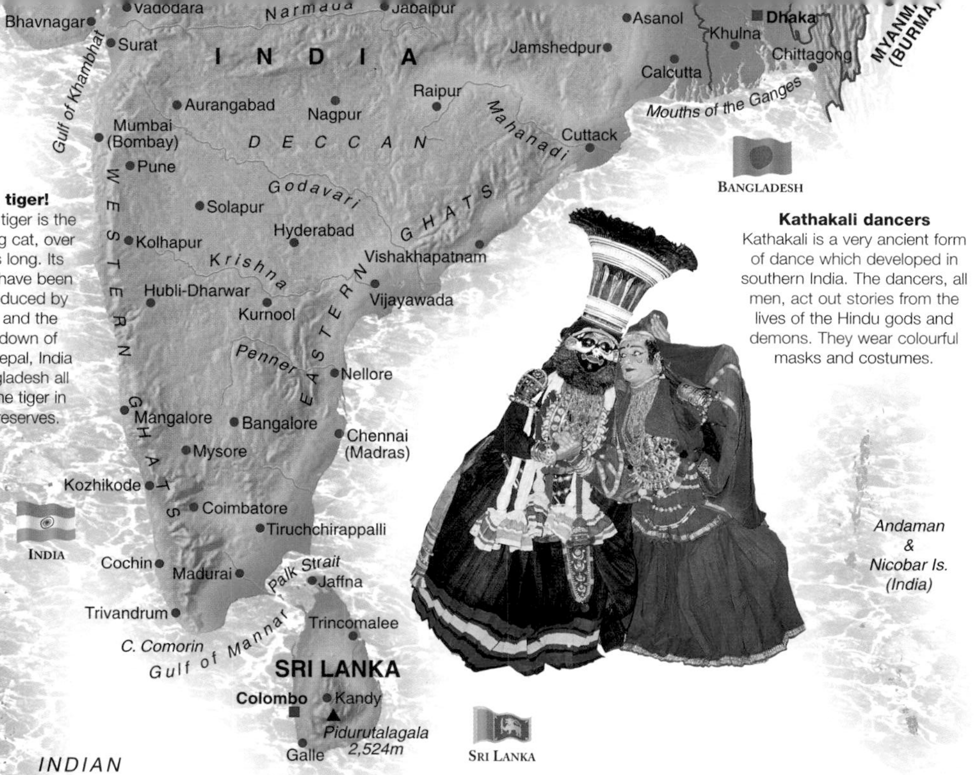

Kathakali dancers

Kathakali is a very ancient form of dance which developed in southern India. The dancers, all men, act out stories from the lives of the Hindu gods and demons. They wear colourful masks and costumes.

Taj Mahal

The domes and gleaming white marble of the Taj Mahal may be seen near the Indian city of Agra. It is often said to be the world's most beautiful building. It is a tomb which commemorates Mumtaz Muhal, the wife of ruler Shah Jehan, and was completed in 1653.

FACT BOX

◆ **Afghanistan**
Area: 652,225 sq km
Population: 22,100,000
Capital: Kabul
Official languages: Pushtu, Dari
Currency: Afghani

◆ **Bangladesh**
Area: 144,000 sq km
Population: 122,210,000
Capital: Dhaka
Official language: Bengali
Currency: Taka

◆ **Bhutan**
Area: 46,620 sq km
Population: 800,000
Capital: Thimphu
Official languages: Dzongkha, English
Currency: Ngultrum

◆ **India**
Area: 3,166,830 sq km
Population: 969,700,000
Capital: Delhi
Official languages: Hindi, Assamese, Bengali, Gujarati, Kannarese, Kashmiri, Malayalam, Marathi, Oriya, Punjabi, Sanskrit, Sindhi, Tamil, Telugu, Urdu, Nepali
Currency: Indian rupee

◆ **Maldives**
Area: 298 sq km
Population: 300,000
Capital: Malé
Official language: Divehi
Currency: Rufiyaa

◆ **Nepal**
Area: 141,415m sq km
Population: 22,600,000
Capital: Kathmandu
Official language: Nepali
Currency: Nepalese rupee

◆ **Pakistan**
Area: 803,940 sq km
Population: 137,800,000
Capital: Islamabad
Official language: Urdu
Currency: Pakistani rupee

◆ **Sri Lanka**
Area: 65,610 sq km
Population: 18,700,000
Capital: Colombo
Official language: Sinhalese, Tamil
Currency: Sri Lankan rupee

CHINA AND ITS NEIGHBOURS

CHINA is the world's third largest country in area, and has a higher population than any other. It is bordered by the world's highest mountains, by deserts and by tropical seas.

Most people live in the big industrial cities of the south and east and on the fertile plains around two great rivers, the Huang He and the Chiang Jiang. Crops include wheat, maize, tea, sugar-cane and rice. Rice is eaten with almost every meal.

Chinese civilization dates back over thousands of years. Chinese inventions included paper and gunpowder and Chinese crafts included the making of fine porcelain and silk. Since 1949 China has been ruled by its Communist Party, but its politics are no longer really socialist. Its economy has become one of the most important in the Pacific region, and in 1997 it took back the territory of Hong Kong, an international centre of business which had been a British colony. China also claims the island of **Taiwan**, which is still governed independently by Chinese nationalists who lost power in 1949.

The **Korean peninsula** saw bitter fighting between 1950 and 1953, when Korea divided into two nations, North and South. These countries remain bitter enemies today. South Korea has become an important industrial power.

Far to the north the Mongol peoples live in the independent republic of **Mongolia**. This includes the barren Gobi desert and remote grasslands.

Temple of Heaven
Tiantan, the Temple of Heaven in Beijing, is a beautiful group of buildings first raised in 1420. The Chinese emperors used to come here to pray for a good harvest.

The Great Wall
A defensive wall runs across the north of China for about 6,000 kilometres, with many extra twists and turns. It was started in about 246 BC and added to over hundreds of years.

Xinjiang herders
These herders are from Tangbula in Xinjiang, a remote region about the size of Alaska in China's far west. Xinjiang is home to several different peoples, including Uygurs, Kazakhs and Uzbekis.

FACT BOX

◆ **China**
Area: 9,597,000 sq km
Population: 1,236,700,000
Capital: Beijing
Main language: Standard Chinese
Currency: Yuan

◆ **Taiwan**
Area: 35,990 sq km
Population: 21,500,000
Capital: Taipei
Main language: Standard Chinese
Currency: New Taiwan dollar

◆ **North Korea**
Area: 122,310 sq km
Population: 24,400,000
Capital: Pyongyang
Main language: Korean
Currency: Won

◆ **South Korea**
Area: 98,445 sq km
Population: 45,900,000
Capital: Seoul
Main language: Korean
Currency: Won

◆ **Mongolia**
Area: 1,565,000 sq km
Population: 2,371,000
Capital: Ulan Bator
Official language: Mongolian
Currency: Tugrik

Panda country
The very rare giant panda lives in the misty bamboo forests of southwest China. It feeds mostly upon bamboo shoots, grasses and bulbs.

Rice bowl
The most important crop in China, and feeding a population of over a billion, rice is prepared in many exotic ways. Traditionally eaten with chopsticks Chinese food has become an international favourite.

JAPAN

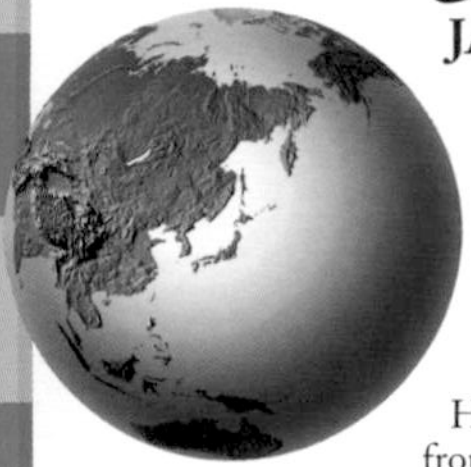

JAPAN is made up of over 3,000 islands, and these stretch for about 3,000 kilometres from north to south on the northwest rim of the Pacific Ocean.

The chief islands are called Hokkaido, Honshu, Shikoku and Kyushu. The islands extend from the tropical south to the chilly north, where winter snowfalls can be heavy. The region is a danger zone for earthquakes and Japan's highest mountain, Fuji, is a volcano.

The snow-covered slopes of Mount Fuji have been a favourite subject for Japanese artists over the years. Japan has a long history of excellence in art, theatre, poetry, architecture and pottery. Japanese civilization dates back over 2,000 years. The country has been ruled by emperors and, during the Middle Ages, it was fought over by powerful warlords and bands of knights called samurai. Faiths include Buddhism and Shinto, the country's traditional religion.

Japan is very mountainous and so land that is suitable for farming is very precious. Japanese farmers grow rice, tea and fruit and the country also has a large fishing fleet. Many meals are based on rice or fish. Japan has very few natural resources. Even so, over the last 50 years Japan has become a leading world producer of cars, televisions and other electrical goods.

The mountains also limit the spread of housing and so Japan's cities are mostly crowded on to the strip of flat land around the coast. Tokyo has spread out to join up with neighbouring cities, and now has a population of over 25 million.

The Japanese people make up 99 percent of the country's population. The remainder includes Koreans and the Ainu of the far north, who may be descended from the first people to inhabit Japan.

Tea time

Tea is harvested on the inland slopes. The Japanese are great tea-drinkers and have an ancient ceremony at which tea is specially prepared and served.

Mount Fuji

The beautiful peak of Mount Fuji, to the southwest of Tokyo, is a national symbol and, traditionally, a sacred mountain.

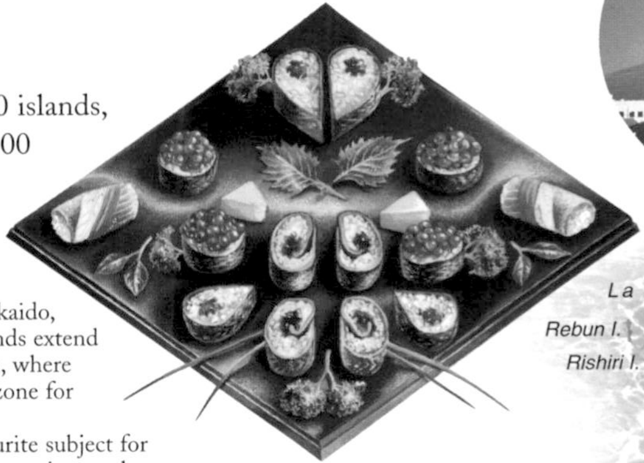

Sushi

Prawns, raw fish, seaweed, pickles and vegetables are used to make these tasty snacks. Like most Japanese dishes, they are served with rice. Japanese food is often beautifully arranged and thoughtfully served.

FACT BOX

◆ **Japan**
Area: 369,700 sq km
Population: 126,100,000
Capital: Tokyo
Main language: Japanese
Currency: Yen

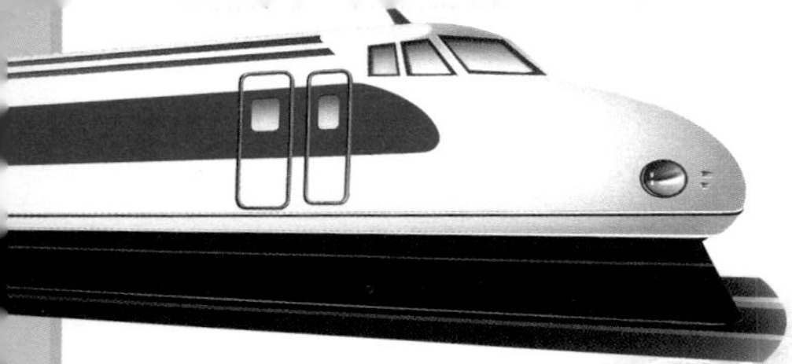

Ride the Bullet

Japan's Bullet Train offers one of the world's most famous passenger express services. It speeds across the country, linking the capital, Tokyo, with other large cities.

Itsukushima, Japan

Japan has many ancient Shinto shrines and Buddhist temples and many of these are set in beautiful scenery or gardens. Japan has always produced very simple and beautiful architecture and design.

A Shinto wedding

Dressed in her beautiful silk robe, or kimono, a Japanese bride sits next to her new husband, who also wears traditional costume. The wedding has been a Shinto ceremony. Shinto is an ancient Japanese faith which honours ancestors and the spirits of nature.

Sumo wrestlers

The ancient sport of sumo is still very popular in Japan. Super heavyweight wrestlers aim to ground their opponents or force them out of the ring. There are long ceremonies before each contest.

SOUTHEAST ASIA

MYANMAR is a beautiful land lying between the hill country of India and China. It is crossed by the great Irrawaddy river, which flows south into the Indian Ocean. To the southeast is **Thailand**, a country green with rice fields and teak forests. To the west lie the lands once known as Indo-China – **Laos**, **Cambodia** and, on the long Mekong River, **Vietnam**.

Linked to the Asian mainland by a narrow isthmus, or strip of land, is **Malaysia**. This country also takes up the northern part of the island of Borneo, which it shares with the small oil-rich state of **Brunei**. Malaysia produces rubber, rice, tea and palm oil. Kuala Lumpur is a growing centre of international business with the 452 metre-high Petronas Towers, the world's highest building. **Singapore**, a small independent city state built on the islands across the Johor Strait, is another leader in the business world.

Indonesia makes up the world's largest island chain. It covers over 13,600 islands, which include Sumatra, Java, southern Borneo, Bali and Irian Jaya (the western half of New Guinea). Another large island chain, the **Philippines**, lie between the Pacific and the South China Sea.

All the islands bordering the Pacific Ocean lie in a danger zone for earthquakes and volcanoes. The region as a whole has a warm, often humid, climate, with monsoon winds bringing heavy rains. Southeast Asia's dwindling tropical forests are a last reserve for the region's rich wildlife, such as enormous butterflies and giant apes called orang-utans.

Many different peoples live in Southeast Asia, including Burmese, Thais, Vietnamese and Filippinos. There are also many people of Chinese and Indian descent. Buddhism is a major faith in the region. Most Indonesians are Muslims and the Philippines are largely Roman Catholic. During the last 50 years Southeast Asia has been torn apart by wars. The region now looks forward to a period of peace.

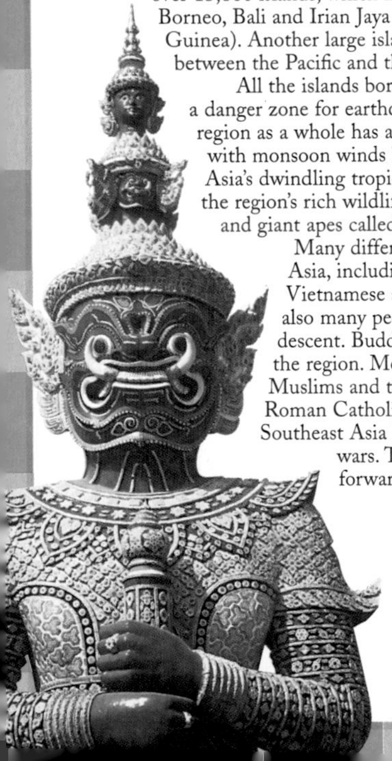

The face of a demon
This fierce-looking demon guards the gate of the Grand Palace in Bangkok, the capital of Thailand. Many tourists come to this kingdom, once known as Siam, to see its ancient temples and enjoy its beautiful scenery and beaches.

A dome of gold
The fantastic roofs of Shwe Dagon pagoda shimmer with gold. This holy site is in Yangon, capital city of Myanmar or Burma. The pagoda honours Gautama Buddha, the founder of the Buddhist faith.

Javanese carving

These beautiful figures, carved from stone, decorate Barobodur, on the island of Java. This 9th-century temple is the most splendid in Indonesia. Its carvings show scenes from the life of the Buddha.

Fact Box

◆ **Myanmar (Burma)**
Area: 678,030 sq km
Population: 46,800,000
Capital: Yangon (Rangoon)
Official language: Myanmar (Burmese)
Currency: Kyat

◆ **Thailand**
Area: 514,000 sq km
Population: 60,100,000
Capital: Bangkok
Official language: Thai
Currency: Baht

◆ **Laos**
Area: 236,725 sq km
Population: 5,100,000
Capital: Vientiane
Official language: Lao
Currency: Kip

◆ **Cambodia**
Area: 181,000 sq km
Population: 11,200,000
Capital: Phnom Penh
Official language: Khmer
Currency: Riel

◆ **Vietnam**
Area: 329,565 sq km
Population: 75,100,000
Capital: Hanoi
Official language: Vietnamese
Currency: Dong

◆ **Malaysia**
Area: 332,965 sq km
Population: 21,000,000
Capital: Kuala Lumpur
Official language: Bahasa Malaysia
Currency: Ringgit (Malay dollar)

◆ **Singapore**
Area: 616 sq km
Population: 3,500,000
Capital: Singapore City
Official languages: English, Chinese, Malay, Tamil
Currency: Singapore dollar

◆ **Indonesia**
Area: 1,919,445 sq km
Population: 204,300,000
Capital: Djakarta
Official language: Bahasa Indonesia
Currency: Rupiah

◆ **Brunei**
Area: 5,765 sq km
Population: 276,000
Capital: Bandar Seri Begawan
Official language: Malay
Currency: Ringgit (Brunei dollar)

◆ **Philippines**
Area: 300,000 sq km
Population: 73,400,000
Capital: Manila
Official language: Filipino
Currency: Peso

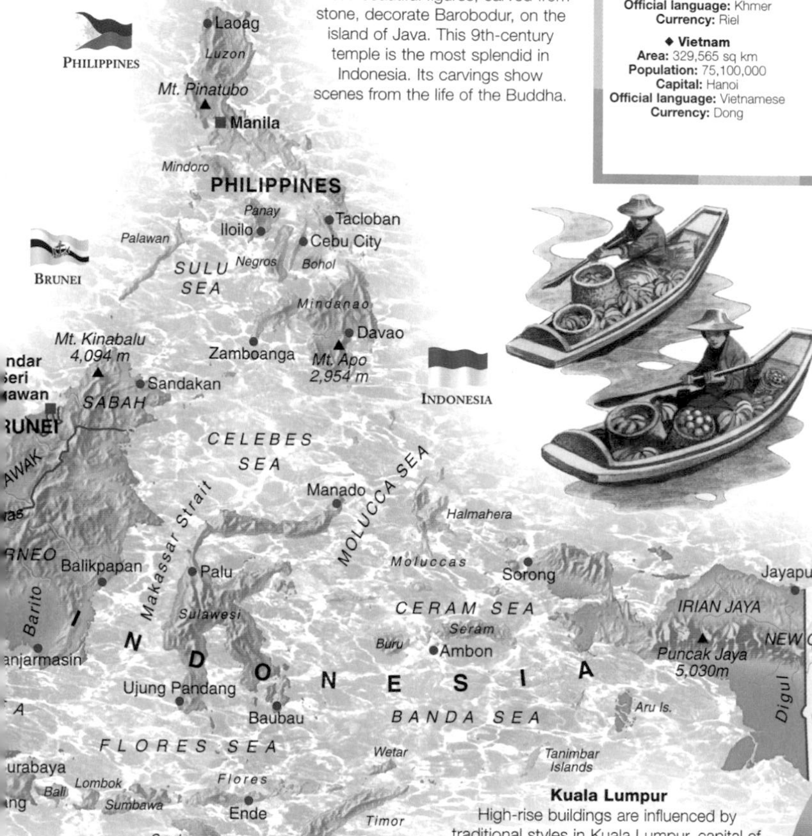

Floating market

At a Thai market, fruit, vegetables or fish may be sold from small boats. These women traders wear broad-brimmed straw hats to protect them from the tropical sun and the heavy monsoon rains.

Kuala Lumpur

High-rise buildings are influenced by traditional styles in Kuala Lumpur, capital of Malaysia. 'KL' is one of the most important centres of industry, and business in Southeast Asia.

Komodo dragon

Meet the biggest lizard in the world, 3 metres long and weighing in at up to 136 kilograms. It is found on four small islands in Indonesia, called Rintja, Flores, Padar and Komodo.

NORTH AND WEST AFRICA

Water for sale
A Berber water seller walks the streets of Marrakech, in Morocco, offering metal cups to passers-by.

THE SAHARA IS THE WORLD'S LARGEST DESERT, made up of over 9 million square kilometres of baking hot sand, gravel and rock.

Its northern fringes, occupied by **Morocco**, **Algeria**, **Tunisia** and **Libya**, run into the milder, more fertile lands of the Mediterranean coast and the Atlas mountain ranges. They are home to Arabs and Berbers.

Deserts stretch from the Sahara eastwards to **Egypt** and the Red Sea. In ancient times one of the greatest civilizations the world has seen grew up in Egypt. Then as now, the country depended on water from the world's longest

river, the Nile. This flows north to the Mediterranean from the mountains of **Ethiopia** and the swamps of southern **Sudan**, Africa's largest country.

The region south of the Sahara is known as the Sahel. It includes **Senegal**, **Mauritania**, **Mali**, **Niger**, **Burkina Faso** and **Chad**. The people include the Fulani, Kanuri and Hausa. The thin grasslands of the Sahel allow cattle herding, but droughts are common and the desert is spreading. Many people are very poor.

Thirteen nations border the great bulge of the West African coast, around the Gulf of Guinea. The coastal strip is made up of lagoons and long sandy beaches fringed with palm trees. Inland there is a belt of forest, which rises to dry, sandy plateaus and semi-desert in the far north. West African history tells of African kingdoms and empires which grew up here long ago, but also of the cruel slave trade across the Atlantic, which lasted from the 1500s to the 1800s. In the 1800s, large areas of West Africa became colonies of Britain and France. Today these lands are independent. The region has rich resources, including oil and diamonds.

Abu Simbel

When the new Aswan dam was being built in the 1960s this great temple of the ancient Egyptian ruler Rameses II had to be moved stone-by-stone

FACT BOX

◆ **Morocco**
Area: 458,730 sq km
Population: 28,200,000
Capital: Rabat
Official language: Arabic
Currency: Dirham

◆ **Western Sahara**
Area: 252,120 sq km
Population: 261,000
disputed territory
Official language: Arabic
Currency: Dirham

◆ **Algeria**
Area: 2,381,745 sq km
Population: 29,800,000
Capital: Algiers
Official language: Arabic
Currency: Algerian dinar

◆ **Tunisia**
Area: 164,150 sq km
Population: 9,300,000
Capital: Tunis
Official language: Arabic
Currency: Tunisian dinar

◆ **Libya**
Area: 1,759,540 sq km
Population: 5,600,000
Capital: Tripoli
Official language: Arabic
Currency: Libyan dinar

◆ **Egypt**
Area: 1,000,250 sq km
Population: 64,800,000
Capital: Cairo
Official language: Arabic
Currency: Egyptian pound

◆ **Sudan**
Area: 2,505,815 sq km
Population: 28,129,000
Capital: Khartoum
Official language: Arabic
Currency: Sudanese pound

◆ **Eritrea**
Area: 91,600 sq km
Population: 3,500,000
Capital: Asmara
Languages: Tigrinya, Amharic
Currency: birr

◆ **Ethiopia**
Area: 1,104,300 sq km
Population: 58,700,000
Capital: Addis Ababa
Official language: Amharic
Currency: Birr

◆ **Djibouti**
Area: 23,200 sq km
Population: 600,000
Capital: Djibouti
Languages: Arabic, French
Currency: Djibouti franc

◆ **Mauritania**
Area: 1,030,700 sq km
Population: 2,400,000
Capital: Nouakchott
Languages: Arabic, French
Currency: Ouguiya

◆ **Mali**
Area: 1,240,140 sq km
Population: 10,137,000
Capital: Bamako
Official language: French
Currency: Franc CFA

◆ **Burkina Faso**
Area: 274,122 sq km
Population: 10,900,000
Capital: Ouagadougou
Official language: French
Currency: Franc CFA

◆ **Niger**
Area: 1,186,410 sq km
Population: 9,800,000
Capital: Niamey
Official language: French
Currency: Franc CFA

◆ **Chad**
Area: 1,284,000 sq km
Population: 7,000,000
Capital: N'Djamena
Languages: Arabic, French
Currency: Franc CFA

◆ **Cameroon**
Area: 475,500 sq km
Population: 13,900,000
Capital: Yaoundé
Languages: English, French
Currency: Franc CFA

◆ **Equatorial Guinea**
Area: 28,050 sq km
Population: 379,000
Capital: Malabo
Official language: Spanish
Currency: Franc CFA

◆ **São Tomé and Príncipe**
Area: 964 sq km
Population: 124,000
Capital: São Tomé
Official language: Portuguese
Currency: Dobra

◆ **Nigeria**
Area: 923,850 sq km
Population: 119,328,000
Capital: Abuja
Official language: English
Currency: Naira

◆ **Benin**
Area: 112,620 sq km
Population: 5,900,000
Capital: Porto-Novo
Official language: French
Currency: Franc CFA

◆ **Togo**
Area: 56,785 sq km
Population: 4,700,000
Capital: Lomé
Official language: French
Currency: Franc CFA

◆ **Ghana**
Area: 238,305 sq km
Population: 18,100,000
Capital: Accra
Official language: English
Currency: Cedi

◆ **Ivory Coast**
Area: 322,465 sq km
Population: 15,000,000
Capital: Abidjan
Official language: French
Currency: Franc CFA

◆ **Liberia**
Area: 111,370 sq km
Population: 2,640,000
Capital: Monrovia
Official language: English
Currency: Liberian dollar

•**Sierra Leone**
Area: 72,325 sq km
Population: 4,494,000
Capital: Freetown
Official language: English
Currency: Leone

◆ **Guinea**
Area: 245,855 sq km
Population: 7,500,000
Capital: Conakry
Official language: French
Currency: Guinean franc

◆ **Guinea-Bissau**
Area: 36,125 sq km
Population: 1,028,000
Capital: Bissau
Official language: Portuguese
Currency: Guinea-Bissau peso

◆ **Gambia**
Area: 10,690 sq km
Population: 1,200,000
Capital: Banjul
Official language: English
Currency: Dalasi

◆ **Senegal**
Area: 196,720 sq km
Population: 8,800,000
Capital: Dakar
Official language: French
Currency: Franc CFA

◆ **Cape Verde Islands**
Area: 4,035 sq km
Population: 395,000
Capital: Praia
Official language: Portuguese
Currency: Cape Verde escudo

CENTRAL, EASTERN & SOUTHERN AFRICA

CENTRAL AFRICA is dominated by the river Congo, which flows through hot and humid rainforest to the Atlantic Ocean. The great river winds through the **Democratic Republic of the Congo**, and the network of waterways which drain into it provide useful transport routes for riverboats and canoes.

A long crack in the Earth's crust, the Great Rift Valley, runs all the way down **East Africa**. Its route is marked by volcanoes and lakes. Some East African mountains remain snow-capped all year round, even though they are on the Equator. The highest of these is Kilimanjaro, at 5,950 metres. It looks out over savanna, grasslands dotted with trees. Huge herds of wildlife roam these plains. Zebra, giraffe, elephants and lions are protected within national parks. The Indian Ocean coast includes white beaches and coral islands. Mombasa, Dar-es-Salaam and Maputo are major ports.

In southern Africa the Drakensberg mountains descend to grassland known as veld. There are harsh deserts too, the Kalahari and the Namib. The **Republic of South Africa** is one of the most powerful countries in Africa. It has ports at Durban and Capetown.

Central and southern Africa are rich in mineral resources, including gold, diamonds and copper. Eastern and southern Africa are important farming regions, raising cattle and producing coffee, vegetables, tropical fruits, tobacco, and grape vines.

African kingdoms flourished in the Congo region in the Middle Ages and the stone ruins of Great Zimbabwe recall gold traders of long ago. Today the region is home to hundreds of African peoples with many different languages and cultures.

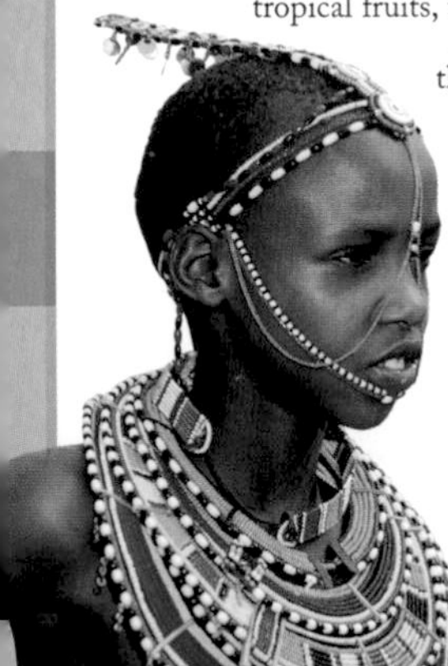

Magnificent Masai
This young Masai girl wears her traditional beaded necklace and headdress. These noble, nomadic people herd cattle and live mainly in Kenya and Tanzania.

La Digue, Seychelles
Over 100 islands make up the Seychelles. La Digue is only 15 square kilometres in area, but the third most populated.

Sting in the tail
Scorpions always look threatening. The curled-forward tail contains a sting which can be deadly. They eat insects and other animals which they catch with their claws. They are most common in desert areas.

FACT BOX

◆ **Central African Republic**
Area: 624,975 sq km
Population: 3,300,000
Capital: Bangui
Main language: French
Currency: Franc CFA

◆ **Gabon**
Area: 267,665 sq km
Population: 1,200,000
Capital: Libreville
Main language: French
Currency: Franc CFA

◆ **Republic of Congo**
Area: 342,000 sq km
Population: 2,500,000
Capital: Brazzaville
Main language: French
Currency: Franc CFA

◆ **Democratic Republic of Congo (Zaïre)**
Area: 2,345,410 sq km
Population: 46,500,000
Capital: Kinshasa
Main language: French
Currency: Zaire

◆ **Rwanda**
Area: 26,330 sq km
Population: 6,900,000
Capital: Kigali
Main languages: Kinyarwanda, French
Currency: Rwanda franc

◆ **Burundi**
Area: 27,835 sq km
Population: 5,900,000
Capital: Bujumbura
Main languages: Kirundi, French
Currency: Burundi franc

◆ **Uganda**
Area: 236,580 sq km
Population: 22,000,000
Capital: Kampala
Main language: English
Currency: Uganda shilling

◆ **Kenya**
Area: 582,645 sq km
Population: 28,200,000
Capital: Nairobi
Main languages: Swahili, English
Currency: Kenya shilling

◆ **Somalia**
Area: 630,000 sq km
Population: 9,500,000
Capital: Mogadishu
Main languages: Somali, Arabic
Currency: Somali shilling

◆ **Tanzania**
Area: 939,760 sq km
Population: 29,100,000
Capital: Dodoma
Main languages: Swahili, English
Currency: Tanzanian shilling

◆ **Seychelles**
Area: 404 sq km
Population: 100,000
Capital: Victoria
Official languages: English, French, Creole
Currency: Seychelles rupee

◆ **Comoros**
Area: 1,860 sq km
Population: 600,000
Capital: Moroni
Official languages: Arabic, French
Currency: Comorian franc

◆ **Mauritius**
Area: 1,865 sq km
Population: 1,100,000
Capital: Port Louis
Official language: English

◆ **Madagascar**
Area: 594,180 sq km
Population: 15,200,000
Capital: Antananarivo
Official languages: Malagasy, French
Currency: Malagasy franc

◆ **Mozambique**
Area: 784,755sq km
Population: 16,500,000
Capital: Maputo
Official language: Portuguese
Currency: Metical

◆ **Malawi**
Area: 94,080 sq km
Population: 9,500,000
Capital: Lilongwe
Official language: Chichewa, English
Currency: Kwacha

◆ **Zambia**
Area: 752,615 sq km
Population: 9,200,000
Capital: Lusaka
Official language: English
Currency: Kwacha

◆ **Zimbabwe**
Area: 390,310 sq km
Population: 11,500,000
Capital: Harare
Official language: English
Currency: Zimbabwe dollar

◆ **Botswana**
Area: 575,000 sq km
Population: 1,500,000
Capital: Gaborone
Official language: English
Currency: Pula

◆ **Lesotho**
Area: 30,345 sq km
Population: 2,100,000
Capital: Maseru
Official languages: Sesotho, English
Currency: Loti

◆ **Swaziland**
Area: 17,365 sq km
Population: 1,000,000
Capital: Mbabane
Official languages: Swazi, English
Currency: Lilangeni

◆ **South Africa**
Area: 1,220,845 sq km
Population: 44,500,000
Capitals: Pretoria, Cape Town
Official languages: Afrikaans, English, Ndebele, Sesotho, Swazi, Tsonga, Tswana, Venda, Xhodsa, Zulu
Currency: Rand

◆ **Namibia**
Area: 824,295 sq km
Population: 1,600,000
Capital: Windhoek
Official language: English
Currency: Namibian dollar

◆ **Angola**
Area: 1,246,700 sq km
Population: 11,500,000
Capital: Luanda
Official language: Portuguese
Currency: Kwanza

AUSTRALIA

THIS COUNTRY is the size of a continent, a huge mass of land surrounded by ocean. The heart of **Australia** is a vast expanse of baking desert, salt pans, shimmering plains and dry scrubland. Ancient, rounded rocks glow in the morning and evening sun.

These barren lands are fringed by grasslands, tropical forests, creeks and fertile farmland. In the far east is the Great Dividing Range, which rises to the high peaks of the Australian Alps. The southeast is crossed by the Murray and Darling rivers. The Great Barrier Reef, the world's largest coral reef, stretches for over 2,000 kilometres off the eastern coast, while the island of Tasmania lies to the south across the Bass Strait.

Most Australians don't live in the 'outback', the dusty back country with its huge sheep and cattle stations and its mines. They live in big coastal cities such as Brisbane, Sydney, Adelaide and Perth. There they enjoy a high standard of living, an outdoor lifestyle, sunshine and surfing.

To the many people who in recent years have come from Europe and Asia to settle in Australia, this seems like a new country. However it is really a very ancient land, cut off from other parts of the world so long that it has many animals seen nowhere else on Earth, such as kangaroos, echidnas and platypuses.

Australia has probably been home to Aboriginal peoples for over 50,000 years. European settlement began in 1788, when the British founded a prison colony at Botany Bay, near today's city of Sydney. Many Australians still like to keep in touch with British relatives and traditions, but the modern country follows its own path as one of the great economic powers of the Pacific region.

Opera on the harbour
Sydney's most famous landmark is its Opera House, built between 1959 and 1973. It rises from the blue waters of the harbour like a great sailing ship. Sydney, the capital of New South Wales, is Australia's biggest city with a population of about 3,700,000.

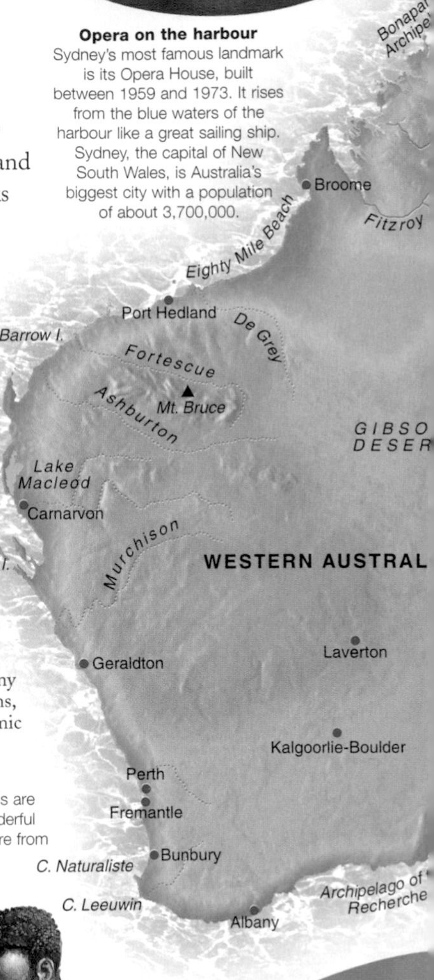

Christmas beetles
Australia and its surrounding islands are popuated by many weird and wonderful insects and beetles. These beetles are from Christmas Island.

Aboriginal art
An Aboriginal artist from Groote Eylandt, an island in the Gulf of Carpentaria, completes a painting on bark. Paintings by Australia's Aborigines are admired around the world. They often recall the ancient myths and legends of their people, with bold, swirling patterns or pictures of animals.

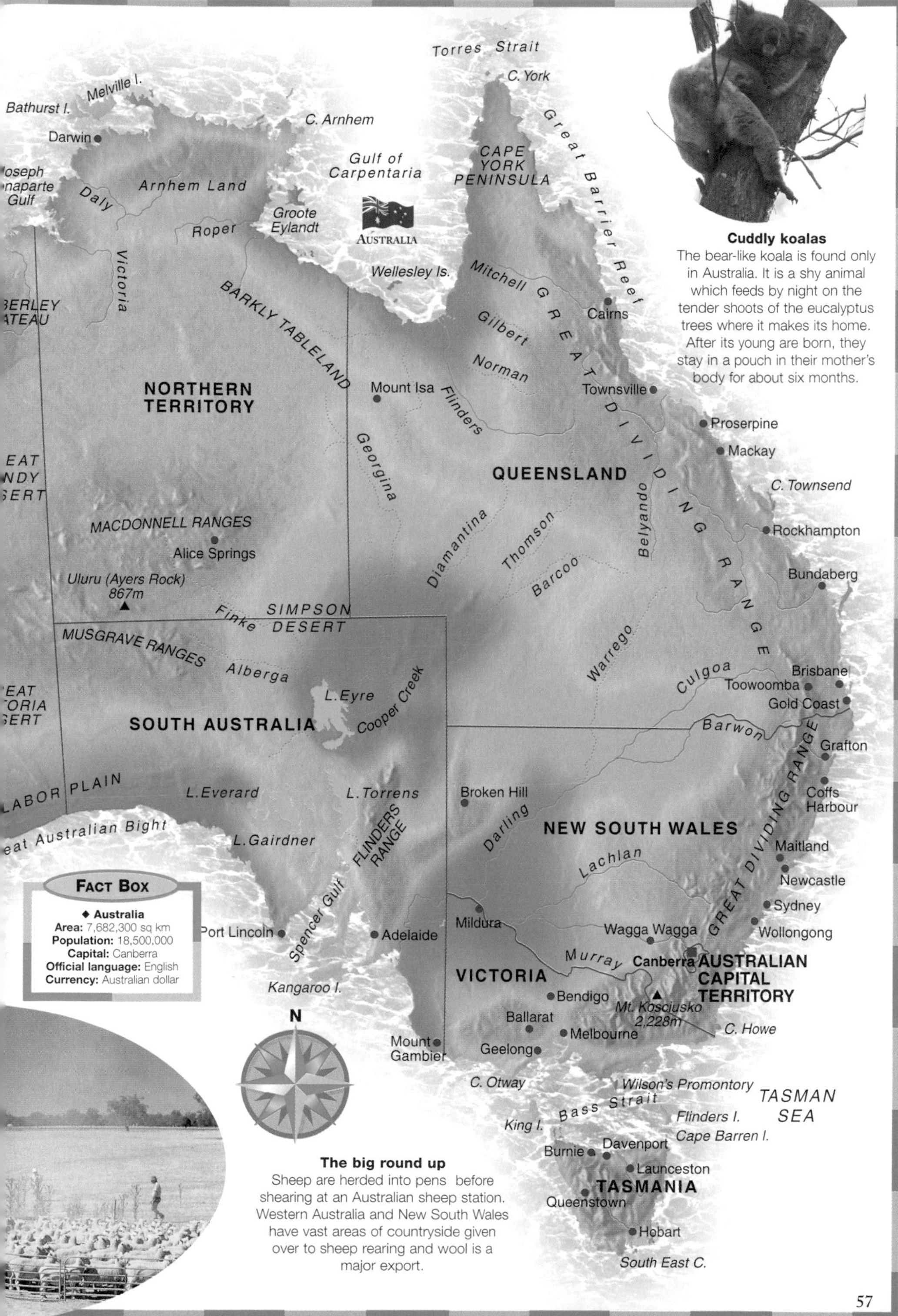

Cuddly koalas
The bear-like koala is found only in Australia. It is a shy animal which feeds by night on the tender shoots of the eucalyptus trees where it makes its home. After its young are born, they stay in a pouch in their mother's body for about six months.

FACT BOX

◆ **Australia**
Area: 7,682,300 sq km
Population: 18,500,000
Capital: Canberra
Official language: English
Currency: Australian dollar

The big round up
Sheep are herded into pens before shearing at an Australian sheep station. Western Australia and New South Wales have vast areas of countryside given over to sheep rearing and wool is a major export.

NEW ZEALAND AND THE PACIFIC

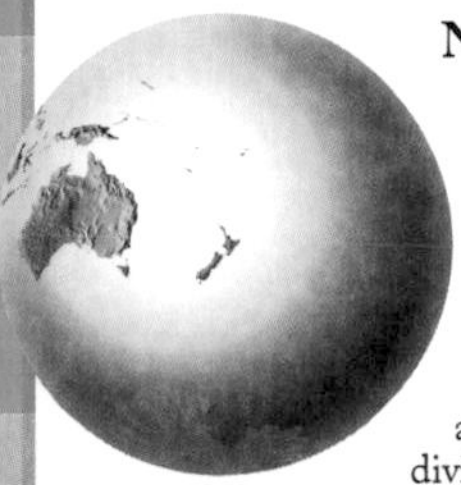

NEW ZEALAND LIES in the Pacific Ocean, about 1,600 kilometres to the east of Australia. It has a moist, mild climate and many unusual plants, birds and animals may be found there.

Most of its people live on North Island and South Island. These beautiful islands, divided by the Cook Strait, are the largest of several which are included within the country. North Island has volcanoes, hot springs and gushing geysers. South Island is dominated by the peaks and glaciers of the Southern Alps. It also has deep sea inlets called fiords and rolling grassy plains. New Zealand, with its sheep, cattle and fruit farms, has one of the most important economies in the Pacific region.

Papua New Guinea is another island nation, bordering Indonesian territory on the island of New Guinea. It also includes several chains of smaller islands. Many of its mountain regions, blanketed in tropical forests, were only opened up to the outside world in the 20th century. The country is rich in mineral resources and its fertile soils produce coffee, tea and rubber.

Strung out eastwards across the lonely Pacific Ocean are many scattered island chains and reefs. Small coral islands surround peaceful blue lagoons ringed with palm trees. The islanders may make their living by fishing, growing coconuts, mining or tourism. Many of the island groups have banded together to form independent nation states.

Peoples of the Pacific are of varied descent. Some are the descendants of European settlers - for example the British in New Zealand, or the French on New Caledonia or Tahiti. Fiji has a large population of Indian descent. The original peoples of the Pacific fall into three main groups. Melanesians, such as the Solomon Islanders, live in the western Pacific, while Micronesians live in the Caroline and Marshall Islands. The Polynesian peoples, brilliant seafarers, colonized vast areas of the oceans, from New Zealand to the Hawaiian Islands. The Maoris, who make up nine percent of New Zealand's population, are a Polynesian people who have kept and valued many of their ancient traditions.

New Guinea finery
Feathers and paint are worn by many young warriors at tribal gatherings and feasts in remote areas of Papua New Guinea. The country has a very rich culture with over 860 different languages.

Kiwi fruit
When farmers decided to grow this fruit in New Zealand, they decided to give it a local name to help sales. The kiwi is the national bird, and a nickname for a New Zealander.

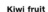

BERING SEA
Papua New Guinea
Palau
NORTH PACIFIC OCEAN
Midway Island (USA)
ake Island (USA)
Marshall Islands
Hawaii (USA)
Vanuatu
arshall Island
Kiribati
Nauru
uru
Kiribati
Samoa
Galapagos (Ecuador)
Tuvalu
Tuvalu
SOUTH PACIFIC OCEAN
Samoa
American Samoa
nuatu
Fiji
French Polynesia
Caledonia France)
Tonga
Cook Islands (New Zealand)
Pitcairn Island (UK)
Easter Island (Chile)
New Zealand
Fiji
Tonga
NEW ALAND

FACT BOX

◆ Papua New Guinea
Area: 462,840 sq km
Population: 4,400,000
Capital: Port Moresby
Official language: English
Currency: Kina

◆ New Zealand
Area: 265,150 sq km
Population: 3,600,000
Capital: Wellington
Official language: English
Currency: New Zealand dollar

◆ Palau
Area: 490 sq km
Population: 16,000
Capital: Koror
Official languages: Palauan, English
Currency: US dollar

◆ Marshall Islands
Area: 181 sq km
Population: 52,000
Capital: Majuro
Official languages: Marshallese, English
Currency: US dollar

◆ Solomon Islands
Area: 29,790 sq km
Population: 354,000
Capital: Honiara
Official language: English
Currency: Solomon Islands dollar

◆ Tuvalu
Area: 25 sq km
Population: 13,000
Capital: Funafuti
Official languages: Tuvaluan, English
Currency: Australian dollar

◆ Kiribati
Area: 684 sq km
Population: 75,000
Capital: Bairiki
Official language: English
Currency: Australian dollar

◆ Nauru
Area: 21 sq km
Population: 10,000
Capital: Yaren
Official language: Nauruan
Currency: Australian dollar

◆ Fiji
Area: 18,330 sq km
Population: 758,000
Capital: Suva
Official language: English
Currency: Fiji dollar

◆ Tonga
Area: 699 sq km
Population: 103,000
Capital: Nukualofa
Official languages: Tongan, English
Currency: Pa'anga

◆ Vanuatu
Area: 14,765 sq km
Population: 156,000
Capital: Porta-Vila
Official languages: Bislama, English, French
Currency: Vatu

◆ Western Samoa
Area: 2,840 sq km
Population: 170,000
Capital: Apia
Official languages: Samoan, English
Currency: Tala

◆ Federated States of Micronesia
Area: 702 sq km
Population: 114,000
Capital: Kolonia
Official language: English
Currency: US dollar

Easter Island
Hundreds of huge, mysterious stone heads tower above the hills of Easter Island, in the eastern Pacific. They were erected by Polynesians about 1,000 years ago. Today Easter Island is governed by Chile.

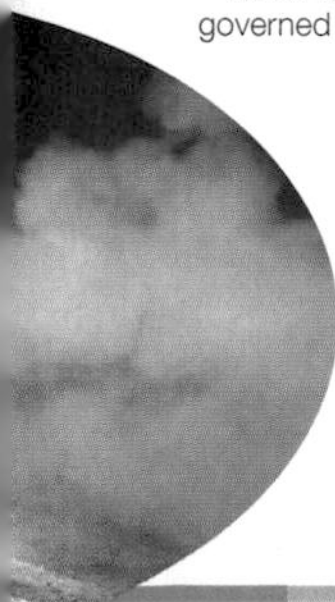

Gusher!
Steam bursts from volcanic rocks near Rotorua on North Island. New Zealand's geysers and hot springs are not just a tourist attraction. They are used to generate electricity.

NEW ZEALAND
North Cape
Whangerei
Gt. Barrier Island
Auckland
Manukau
Bay of Plenty
East Cape
Hamilton
Waikato
Rotorua
NORTH ISLAND
L. Taupo
Gisborne
New Plymouth
Ruapehu 2,797m
Napier
Hastings
Wanganui
Cape Farewell
Palmerston North
Cook Strait
Nelson
Wellington
Westport
Blenheim
Greymouth
SOUTHERN ALPS
SOUTH ISLAND
Canterbury Plains
Christchurch
Mt.Cook 3,764m
Timaru
Clutha
Dunedin
Foveaux Strait
Invercargill
Stewart Island
N

POLAR LANDS

Living in the Arctic
The Inuit peoples of northern Canada and Greenland have always lived by hunting and fishing and are experts at surviving in the harsh climate.

THE NORTHERNMOST PART of our globe is called the Arctic. Within this bitterly cold region lie the northern borders of Alaska (part of the United States), Canada, Greenland (a self-governing territory of Denmark), Norway, Sweden, Finland and Russia.

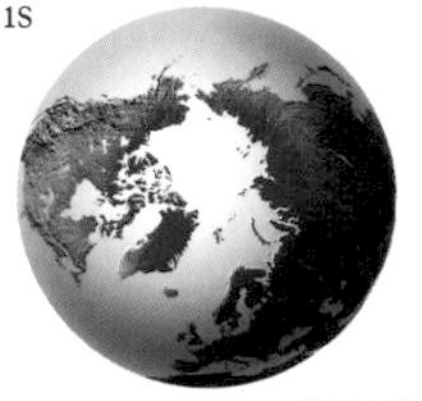

However most of the area is covered by the Arctic Ocean, much of which is frozen solid all year round. At the centre of this great cap of ice is the North Pole. The **Arctic** supports a surprisingly wide selection of wildlife, including seals, walruses and polar bears. Peoples who have learned to live permanently in the far north include the Aleuts, the Inuit, the Saami, the Yakuts and the Chukchi. They have been joined in recent years by workers from the oil industry.

The only people to be found in **Antarctica**, at the other end of the globe, are scientists studying the weather and rocks of the coldest and windiest continent on Earth. The only other living things to survive here are the penguins which breed around the coast and the whales, birds and fishes of the Southern Ocean. The landmass is ringed by a shelf of ice, some of which breaks away to form massive icebergs in the spring. Inland there are mountain ranges and icy plains. The Antarctic winter takes place during the Arctic summer, and the Antarctic summer during the Arctic winter.

Various countries claim territory in Antarctica, and the continent is rich in minerals and fishing. However many scientists argue that this land should never be opened up to mining and industry, but left as the planet's last true wilderness.

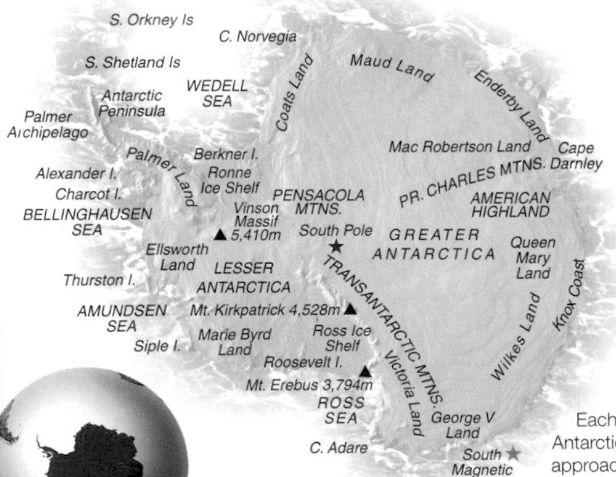

Antarctic melt
Each southern spring, the ice around Antarctica begins to melt, allowing ships to approach the ice shelves around this huge, frozen continent.

FACT BOX

◆ **Arctic Circle**
Area of ocean:
14,056,000 sq km

◆ **Antarctic Circle**
Area of land:
13,900,000 sq km

INDEX

INDEX

Page numbers in *italics* refer to illustrations.

The publishers wish to thank the artists who have contributed to this book:
Julie Banyard; Martin Camm; Mike Foster; Josephine Martin; Terry Riley; Guy Smith; Roger Smith; Michael White/Temple Rogers.

The publishers would like to thank the following for supplying photographs for the Atlas

Page 5 (T/R) MKP; 5 (B) PhotoDisc; 6-7, 9, 10-11 all MKP; 12 (C/R) & (B/L) Spectrum Colour Library; 14 (T/R) MKP; (B/L) & (B) The Stock Market; 15 (B) MKP; 17 (C/R) & B/R) The Stock Market; (B) MKP; 18 (B) MKP; (T/R) & (B/R) The Stock Market; 20-21, 24-25 all MKP; 26 (T/C) MKP; (B/C) The Stock Market; 28 (B/C) The Stock Market; 29 (T/R) The Stock Market; 30 both MKP; 32-33 (C) MKP; 33 (C) The Stock Market; 33 (B/R); MKP; 34 (T/L) MKP; 34 (B) The Stock Market; 35 (C) MKP; 37 (T/L) The Stock Market; (B/C) PhotoDisc; 38 (B/L) MKP; 39 (T/R) PhotoDisc; (C) & (B/R) The Stock Market; 40-41 all Sue Cunningham Photographic; 42-43 all MKP; 44 (T/L) MKP; 45 (C/R) The Stock Market; (B) MKP; 46 (T/R) The Stock Market; (B) & (B/C) MKP; 47 (C/R) MKP; 48 (T/R) & (C) MKP; 49 (C/R) MKP; (B/C) The Stock Market; 50-51 all MKP; 52-53 all MKP; 54-55 all The Stock Market; 56 (T/R) & (B/L) MKP; (B/C) The Stock Market; 58-59, 60-61 all MKP